PET SHOP BOYS: INTROSPECTIVE

75p

PET SHOP BOYS
INTROSPECTIVE

MICHAEL COWTON

SIDGWICK & JACKSON
LONDON

First published in Great Britain in 1991
by Sidgwick & Jackson Limited
18–21 Cavaye Place, London SW10 9PG

Copyright © 1991 by Michael Cowton

All rights reserved. No part of this publication may be reproduced, stored in a retrieval system, or transmitted in any form or by any means, electronic, mechanical, photocopying or otherwise, without the prior written permission of the publisher.

Typeset by Florencetype Ltd, Kewstoke, Avon
Printed in Great Britain by Mackays of Chatham
for Sidgwick & Jackson Limited

Jacket picture acknowledgements

Front: Rex Features
Back: Redferns

Contents

Acknowledgements		vii
Prologue		viii
1	Can You Hear the Dawn Break?	1
2	A Lowe Profile	12
3	The Bobby O Story	18
4	Carrot Cake and a Recording Deal	25
5	What's in a Name?	32
6	The Million Dollar Man?	39
7	Let's Make Lots of Money	47
8	New Opportunities	51
9	Rudest Men in Rock	55
10	Paninaro Poseurs	62
11	They've Got it Taped	68
12	The King and Us	72
13	The Springfield Connection	82
14	Actually . . . It's Brilliant	87
15	It Couldn't Happen Here	92
16	Season of Bad Will	105
17	Rumours and Liza Minnelli	117
18	A Life on the Open Road	125
19	The Piglets of the Eighties	147
20	Memories are Made of This	154
21	Here We Go Round Again	159
Epilogue		163
Notes and Sources		175
Discography		188

Acknowledgements

I extend my grateful thanks to the following people who made this book possible and come to life: my editor at Sidgwick & Jackson, Karen Hurrell, for her constant patience and prompting; Jenny Stevenson, my research assistant and confidante, for her unswerving loyalty, enthusiasm and encouragement (this is for you); the elusive Bobby Orlando, who deserves a book on himself; the bubbly Barbara Windsor; Gareth Hunt; Jonathan King; Tanita Tikaram; Frank Keegan; Robin Duke; Mat Smith; Kevin Feddy; and, Rick Sullivan for the jacket design. To all others whom I have failed to mention, I thank you, too.

Prologue

The Pet Shop Boys never intended to be stars. Even today, with smash singles and albums in their wake, they don't class themselves as operating in the superstar zone. Then again, if this were the case, with whom would you pigeonhole them? Elton John? Bruce Springsteen? The Rolling Stones? Paul McCartney? No. The Pet Shop Boys are small fry compared to these mega merchants, yet they have rightfully earned a place in the pop archives. Perhaps not so much as icons, more as iconoclasts. Not that pop's odd couple deliberately set out to destroy or even compromise all that is statute in the pop industry. From the very beginning, it was if Neil Tennant and Chris Lowe took delight in doing everything against the grain, or rather doing nothing with the grain. After various jump starts, it was not until 1989 that they eventually hit the road, taking their Euro-disco music to the people who had placed them at the very top of the chart tree. And this was only for a mere handful of dates in Hong Kong, Japan and Britain.

Somehow, the Pet Shop Boys metamorphosed into the Pet Shop Ploys with their camp aloofness. They managed to pull the shutters down and shut up shop on their privacy even before their names were abroad – private musicians who refused to share their private lives with a public itching to know more. Maybe it was their game plan to ruffle the feathers of the Press and the public. The Boys successfully managed to stick their own noses in the air, while at the same time rubbing the media's noses in the dirt whenever the latter tried to chisel away at their growing wall of indifference. The duo's insouciance was galling. They were building their reputations on a game of hide-and-seek and only the petulant Pets knew the rules. The media's predatorial snapping almost grew to be a biological impulse.

Without a doubt the chief manipulator was Neil Tennant. He had played on the other side of tracks. As assistant editor of the teen magazine *Smash Hits*, he was well practised in the art of puncturing holes in prima donnas. He knew all the dodges. He had interviewed the stars, he knew the right trap questions to ask, and, whenever they were put to him, he knew how to field them. Then, in 1985, it was he who adopted the starring role of prima donna. He tap-danced his way around the probing set. It proved frustrating for the interviewers – the few that managed to penetrate the net so cleverly cast out by the Boys and their manager, the omnipresent Tom Watkins, who took the brothers Goss, and group friend and bass player Craig Logan from suburban obscurity to international stardom as Bros.

Lowe was happy to admit that the Pet Shop Boys had no star quality; Tennant said that had he still been a journalist, he would see them as big-headed, and difficult people to get on with. Yet, in the early years, he was operating on an extremely flimsy power base. Those media people living under an entertainment anaesthetic were ever-ready to inject poison into their pens when going to press.

One can justifiably question how the Pet Shop Boys became so big, so fast, in a media world which is ever ready to tear down the gossamer-thin veil of stardom that it so willingly drapes around the shoulders of its unsuspecting quarry. What, if anything, were the Boys trying to hide behind their own protective shield? Why were they so bothered that they might dent their reputations, when the only reputation they were building for themselves was one of arrogant indifference? Taunts about their sexuality failed to draw much response from their shells. The sitting Tennant and the Lowe profile were no doubt hurt, but they refused to show it. It seemed that whenever they opened the blinds a crack to let in a sliver of light, they also opened themselves up to the threat of misinterpretation. They preferred not to hint at anything that the media could appropriate, digest and elucidate. 'Obviously people are going to look at our songs and read things into them. Some of them are quite direct, they're written from experience so it's quite embarrassing, really. But we'll never discuss our love lives with the Press. That way, we'll not experience the other side of popularity, that people will offer sums of money for nasty stories on us. It's possible to sell lots of records and still have a private life. Just look at Mark Knopfler, who sells millions of records with Dire Straits but avoids the popular Press. People can still like your records without knowing everything about you,' Tennant once said.

According to him, it was pointless to flaunt the duo across the papers simply because there was a record to plug. Tennant the voice – the bossier of the two and therefore assumed to be the leader. Lowe was more than happy for his partner to take the initiative in all things media. By doing so, he gave a totally wrong impression of himself. Rather than put his foot in it by being too outspoken, he would leave the talking, the diplomatic role, to Tennant, as if he had no opinion. Niggled by questions, Lowe would prefer to hold his silence, rather like a sultry child. As a compromise, he would channel his thoughts through his partner. Lacking in confidence, this could be perceived as Lowe having an inferiority complex. Yet given the chance, usually prompted by Tennant, he would speak his mind, leaving personalities aside.

Static, sombre, sultry, pompous, impersonal and petulant, the adjectives on the duo marched across the music pages like an army of worker ants. The woodentops were taking a hammering and the nails were being driven home by a frustrated Press corps. In some respects, it has been their own fault that they have been misunderstood. The fact is that the irony crept in when they were endeavouring to be serious. This misrepresentation has caused them more embarrassment than upset.

The problem is that their sincerity has been misinterpreted as irony. Tennant, the self-confessed romantic who believed that such romanticism, with its element of hip-hop, hi-NRG, and imagery, seems to him to have been wasted on a non-perceptive public.

That public wanted to know why they didn't tour. There was an easy answer to that one. You only have to watch the videos that expose them as two cardboard cut-outs on stage as the hi-NRG disco beat pumps out its rhythms. Tennant and Lowe were growing to be masters of Euro-pop studio sound technology. Entertainment and self-expression were their lifeline to the industry. They wanted to turn their lack of *joie de vivre* into a mass popular art form. Let the people know that it was fun to be perceived as miserable. There was no message in their music, despite its having a penchant for comment or feelings in the contemporary style. There was nothing macho about what they were writing. To them it was quite straightforward, yet to others it was complicated, maybe even a contradiction. They were obviously giving off the wrong signals, yet chose to carry on in the same vein anyway.

It was glowingly obvious that they would stagnate unless they tried something completely different on stage. The duo Soft Cell, and other contemporary solo keyboard instrumentalists, like Nik Kershaw and Howard Jones, had mastered the art of being stuck behind racks of synthesizers. Basically, they moved. Chris Lowe never would. A taste for trendy shades and a nice line in baseball caps was not going to prove enough to fool a perceptive public and the media critics, whose claws were flexed for action. Tennant, to his credit, was more than happy to admit the duo's limitations over live work. Cocooned in their private world, they said they had nothing to hide or to be ashamed of, and it was true. But that is not what the fans wanted to hear. And, by remaining closeted away from public scrutiny, they were obvious cannon fodder. Tennant may have been well versed in the pop clichés, but playing such a role so closely to his chest, living a life of self-imposed exile from the stage and a public that wanted to see them in the flesh, obviously preyed on his and Chris's minds.

There were several stop-start attempts at getting a show on the road, but finances, or a lack of them, saw the plans grind to a halt. For the Pet Shop Boys kept insisting they had big plans which would cost an awful lot of money. Money they insisted they didn't have. They did not want to put on anything as obvious as a concert, more a variety spectacular, with a dancing troupe, film projected on to a backcloth, and wonderfully bizarre costumes. All well and good, but in the meantime, the public had to satisfy itself with mean, moody photographs of the twosome. It did not end there. They had grown accustomed to fending off the brickbats, but they were not afraid occasionally to knock their peers in the Press. They happily savaged bands.

Pop's most unlikely pair of stars have achieved amazing success since the release of 'West End Girls', with Number One hits, platinum albums, top music awards and well-earned platitudes in their wake. No matter how much they have annoyed people with their attitude, the Pet Shop Boys have deserved their success. They have always taken their work seriously, and have guided their careers with expert precision. No matter what else may be said, no one but Neil Tennant and Chris Lowe have been working the strings of these Pets. They are two stars with the Midas touch who were hailed as the success of the Eighties. Yet, even today, you could walk straight past them in the street without realizing who they are. Naturally, this is all to their liking. They have lead a quiet, reserved life. Self-revelation is not to their liking. They have survived through their isolation and they intend to keep it that way.

One

Can You Hear the Dawn Break?

Neil Francis Tennant was born to Bill and Sheila Tennant on 10 July 1954, in Brunton Park near Gosforth Park, Northumberland, on England's North East coast. The area lies three miles north of Newcastle along the old A1 road and is typical suburbia with its air of quiet respectability, with tree-lined roads, bungalows and semi-detached houses. Newcastle itself can proudly boast of its pop talent since the Sixties. Two of its most famous sons are Eric Burden, who fronted the Animals, and former Police bass player and vocalist, Sting, who, in fact, attended the same school as Neil – St Cuthbert's Catholic Grammar (today called St Cuthbert's High School), which lies to the top of Banwell Hill, enclosed by a high stone wall.

Neil showed a definite leaning towards the arts rather than scientific subjects. He was a studious type, keeping his head burrowed in books rather than becoming actively involved on the sports field. Recalls the head of history at the school, Frank Keegan, 'He was much better on the arts side. I don't think he had much numerical ability.' Frank remembers Neil as an affable boy, who was extremely hard working and particularly interested in history. 'I always remember giving an exercise on Thomas à Beckett and Henry II, and the struggle with the Church. I asked the boys to write a composition, expecting between two and three pages from most of the class. I think Neil wrote eight pages. It was an enormous essay – long without really being well planned. It was the sort of essay you get from people who are enthusiastic without really putting their minds into it. I also remember Neil's writing being rather scrawly.'

Frank Keegan never found Neil difficult to deal with: 'If I had any criticism of him it was that his spelling and his grammar were not consistent with the effort he was putting in. He could have improved on that, but I would not have any quarrels with him on the effort he put in.'

Neil was a bright pupil in class and could stand his ground in most discussion groups, always prepared to put forward interesting ideas. It was a disappointment, then, says Frank Keegan, that he should under-perform at the A-Level stage, his results not being representative of his term work. Neil's downfall was reading subject matter, and analytical work. In 1972, he gained a D in A-Level English, a C in History, and a P in Economics and Public Affairs.

Remembers Frank Keegan; 'Sting was the same. I can never remember him being in trouble either. He was far more interested in sport than Neil. I used to help with athletics and the cross-country teams, and Sting was an excellent athlete, where I can't remember Neil representing the school in any team games. His interests lay with drama and music, and I believe he was involved in a production of Gilbert and Sullivan's *HMS Pinafore* as a young boy.'

In fact, Neil first took an interest in music when his parents purchased a piano for his sister, Susan, who is two years his senior. He also has two brothers – Simon, an accountant and four years younger, and Philip. 'We sent Susan to piano lessons, then Neil took an interest, but he taught himself. He then bought himself a guitar and played in a group called Dust with his friends at Newcastle Festival,' remembers his father, Bill.

Neil joined St Cuthbert's in 1965, and gained an excellent conduct record, collecting As (excellent), A-minuses, Bs (good) and B-minuses throughout his time. His younger brother Philip, who gained an E in Economics at A-Level, was of similar ability and performance, only dropping down to one C (satisfactory) throughout his time at St Cuthbert's.

During his last couple of years at school, Neil spent his summer holidays earning money rather than hanging around on street corners with the rest of the boys, watching the girls go by. One summer found him working as a lift attendant. Another summer he worked behind the counter for Ladbrokes, the bookmakers, in the Percy Street branch, near the Haymarket, Newcastle. Not that he was ever into racing or gambling. . . . He was later to work for Ladbrokes again after his move to London.

Neil was never that popular with other boys at school; he tended to keep to himself. He always looked upon himself as an outsider and admits to having hated attending school for that reason. This was a feeling he continued to entertain during his time at polytechnic, before his tolerance eventually won ground. It was as if this attitude, this indifferent air was a shield, protecting him from other influences and ideals. His defence was that he was somehow different. This stance of moral superiority would be echoed later, in what the Pet Shop Boys were to become. No doubt, if he had given others at school a chance, if he had let down these barriers, he would have found it a more pleasant experience, to be a part of something, to belong, rather than live in his solitary world. Confrontations were obviously not for the young Tennant, and it is therefore understandable that other pupils were puzzled by him.

Never being one of the gang extended to sport, which he loathed. He never excelled at football, possibly the most popular sport in the North East. His loathing for anything to do with sport sometimes found him absent without leave on sports afternoons, when he would meet up with friends from other schools – including the Sacred Heart Convent School, close to St Cuthbert's – those who also classed themselves as outsiders. This clique made a virtue out of their independence and individualism. Friends remember that he took almost a pride in hating sport because it was what the lads did. Because Neil and friends would be skiving while wearing uniforms, they would state that they were on a schools day, if they were ever stopped and questioned. On one such 'awayday' to Denton Park, in Scotswood, the party was chased off by a man with an air rifle. Not that he fired it, but it was enough to send the truants scattering for their lives.

Neil and friends would legitimately meet up after school at the Literary and Philosophical Society, housed near Newcastle's Central Station. Known popularly as the Lit and Phil, Neil was a member of this most imposing of libraries, with its rows upon rows of books, statues and marble pillars. Downstairs was the meeting room, where the teenagers would chat and lark around. Now and again they were told to shut up, but were never thrown out for being too boisterous. Neil took great pride in being a member of such an establishment, which no doubt prompted many of his fellow pupils to look upon him as being somewhat aloof.

Newcastle has changed little since the early Seventies. There are still rough areas, the boys still have their nights on the town, and the girls theirs. For Neil Tennant, the macho image of sleeveless T-shirts, tattoos, pints of beer and the odd fight to round off the evening was never for him. Much of his time was spent at the People's Theatre in Heaton, about two miles out from Newcastle city centre. It boasts an excellent reputation as an amateur theatre, and it gave Neil the opportunity to develop his skills both as a writer and musician, although not so much as an actor.

As part of the Newcastle Festival in 1970 to 1971, the theatre put on three plays, one of which Neil wrote, called *The Baby*. He was also credited with the music for all three, and some of the lyrics. *The Baby* was very much in the teenage-angst mould, about a young couple, of which the girl was pregnant. Having gone through the traumas of explaining the situation to their parents, the couple happily walk off into the sunset to make a new life together. The female lead was played by Barbara Wilson, who has since appeared on various radio plays, and whose biggest claim to fame to date has been her role as one of Eddie Yates's girlfriends in ITV's long-running soap, 'Coronation Street'. The play was shown at the

University Theatre, Newcastle, which was quite a large venue, and it received very good reviews.

Neil preferred not to act in his own play, although he did take a role in a production of *Oliver*. He never landed the lead roles, and seemed happy to wander around in the background as a bit player, like in his role as an orphan in a musical called *Orphans Galore*, about a time when all the parents in the world disappear – almost like a *Lord of the Flies* with music.

Neil is not remembered as being terribly good looking, and he was somewhat gawky, although he had lots of girlfriends – girls who were simply friends. Most members of the theatre company found him interesting; he was more introverted than deep, which is why, no doubt, he preferred to keep in the background and not try for the lead parts. What he did have was a wicked sense of humour, with a tendency to get up to the occasional prank. He had a very quick mind and was quite amusing, but not in a bouncy way; his dry humour could be quite cutting.

In fact, Neil was the last person in the world the company have expected to go on to become a major force in the music industry, particularly as a performer. It was obvious at this time that he was a talented songwriter. Back in those early Seventies, Neil was heavily influenced by the big production numbers of Liza Minnelli and Frank Sinatra, and much of his theatre musical scores leant towards the sophisticated big ballads with their rising chord structures.

Outside of the theatre, Neil stuck to his music and would travel miles to hear new records, particularly those in the hi-NRG vein. In and out of several groups, he enjoyed doing parodies of well-known artists like the Moody Blues and Simon & Garfunkel. He enjoyed sentimentality, yet anything over the top and he would go straight for the jugular.

One of his most successful groups was called Dust, an acoustic folk outfit, influenced by The Incredible String Band. Friends came and went in the group, but the band was fronted vocally by two girls, Pauline Hadaway and Maureen McGarvey (whose father was a leading force in the

Boilermakers' Union). The girls took turns as lead singers. Pauline was a member of the People's Theatre and has since become a successful playwright. She has written for the live theatre company in Newcastle, and her work has been reviewed on the Radio 4 artist programme, 'Kaleidoscope'. Her plays include themes on the miners' strike, a play called *Stitch Up* about employment training and working men's clubs, and *The Dead Sea*, about four women who steal a fishing boat and set off for Spain.

Dust played acoustic numbers, when Neil tried his hand at six-string guitar, of which he proved to be only an average player. But it was enough to get by. Dust would rehearse at its various members' houses, setting up their tape recorder and microphone, and recording Neil's and Pauline's songs. It was more for a laugh than anything else, although Neil did send some of their tapes to Radio Newcastle. This was an odd thing for him to do, as he had never been one to court publicity. The station was so impressed that Dust found themselves in the studio recording six numbers to broadcast over a week-long period on the morning show. One of the local papers gave the members a small mention, stating that the foursome's combined ages totalled sixty-five.

One of Dust's more memorable songs was a ballad composed by Neil entitled 'Can You Hear the Dawn Break?'. No doubt, what they could have heard was a pin drop, when it was suggested that they play a gig at an old folk's place in Scotswood, not a particularly salubrious part of Newcastle. One of their friends' fathers was a member of the Rotary Club, whose responsibility was to organize such social/bingo nights for the senior citizens. Dust was booked as the entertainment at the Sporting Arms public house. As the last call of 'House' rang round the room, the audience put down their pens, tore up their used bingo cards and relaxed while the entertainment began. If they were expecting 'Puff the Magic Dragon', they didn't get it, for Dust launched into a list of self-penned numbers. They collected £10 between them for their efforts.

If nothing else, it was an experience which set them in good stead for their next booking, a night club in Newcastle called Changes. It was the type of place that would have been in its heyday in the Sixties, with lots of noise and one-armed bandits. Hardly the right venue for an acoustic quartet. Dust was more in their element when they entered a talent competition as part of the Newcastle Festival. A stage was erected in Eldon Square, a beautiful old Georgian square which has since been transformed into a shopping centre and park.

Dust played its own material, and was beaten into second place by the number one group in the North East at that time: the Soda Pops, an all-girl group of the Chiffons' mould, from Gramlington. 'We were convinced we would become terribly famous,' says Neil. 'It was very kind of Stoned Seventies, but we used to think it was absolutely brilliant at the time.'

Just as musicians rehearsed with Dust before moving on, so too Dust finally disbanded and later reformed as Ginny Oliver – a North Shields' name for a skate. The fish is believed to act as an aphrodisiac. Neil and friends thought it would be a fun name for the group, which followed a similar path to Dust – no one taking it very seriously.

Consequently, after his successful A-Level results landed through the letterbox, Neil headed south in 1972 to study history at North London Polytechnic in London's Holloway Road, where he was to gain a degree. No doubt, Neil breathed a sigh of relief when he eventually left his home town. London was a world away from the inherent threat of violence that reared its head if you were ever anything but one of the lads. The rough boys versus the theatre camp. It was seen more as a fashion accessory to appear camp, or affected. Not that Neil ever did anything to compromise himself in any way, preferring to keep in the background. But the association stuck. Where camp people would project themselves, prancing around and generally showing off, Neil would be the one in the theatre Green Room, sitting in a corner and looking interesting. Never the first to open his mouth, his detached stance proved an attraction rather than a detraction. Never would he place his heart on his sleeve.

Tennant's musical interests continued in London, when Pauline Hadaway and other Newcastle friends would often turn up at weekends. On one such occasion Neil had arranged for a talent scout from the newly formed Rocket Records to call round at his flat in Mount Pleasant Road, Tottenham. Pauline and a friend from Newcastle called Ingrid had hitched down from the North East, and the night prior to the audition they all went out for a drink. As a result, the following day's performance was dreadful and, naturally, nothing came of it.

Undaunted, Neil continued with his studies, his music, and his exaggerated style of dress. Even at St Cuthbert's, he'd enjoyed winding up the masters about the length of his hair. There was a strict tradition at the school that once a boy's hair reached the top of his collar, he would have to have it cut. The ambition of most boys was to grow it long once they had left. A rebellious afterthought. Neil was one of those who decided to test the tradition, and was occasionally sent home for his trouble.

Neil recalls, 'My major clothes time was in the early seventies. I dyed my hair red. It never recovered from that. I dyed it blond, too. It was quite frightful.' Whenever he returned to Newcastle he would dye it brown again, but this move never fooled his parents. At the height of punk he wore his hair very long. 'I couldn't afford to get it cut. I was working on the *Marvel* Comics getting paid £30 a week and paying £18 a week on my rent so I didn't have much left'. Partner Chris claims he earned more than that washing dishes back home in Blackpool.

Says Neil, 'I had short hair at my college in 1973 when everyone had long hair. And I used to have this major shoe fetish. I used to love wearing high-heeled shoes! Platform shoes weren't right so we used to get women's shoes. The only trouble was that I'm size eight and a half, and the biggest I could get was six and a half. I had to curl up my toes to get them in. I got totally used to it after a year. I can remember walking down the road – it used to kill. Sometimes I used to have to take my shoes off walking down the road when I couldn't stand it any more. I shared a flat with two friends in Tottenham at the time and an old couple lived downstairs. "It's not the noise you make – it's those shoes" they used to say.'

This is probably a slight exaggeration, and Neil is referring to the thick platform shoes so popular in the early Seventies, as opposed to women's stiletto heels. Women's platforms were decidedly more flashy, which is probably what Neil wore; they would have been seen as outrageous in Newcastle, where they were not available in the shops. Neil's flamboyance had certainly taken a turn since his move south. One had to be extremely careful about one's appearance in Newcastle, because so many skinheads roamed the streets waiting for the first opportunity to taunt and punish. If you dressed in anything fashionably unusual, or that could be construed as effeminate – which could be more or less anything – then you were a prime target for a beating: dress sense was all-important.

People even had to be cautious about their drinking venues. The theatre crowd in Newcastle – which included Neil before his move to London – would frequent the Eldon, which has since become a wine bar. At the time, it was known for its gay connections. It was certainly not rough like many of the other hostelries, which is why the theatre crowd enjoyed it so much. You could sit, drink and relax without aggravation. This was at a time when gays were coming out of every closet, and an enormous scene grew in Newcastle, like other major British cities. No heart throb, Neil was popular with girls, although he was never interested to the extent of chasing them like other boys, which is possibly why some people assumed he was gay. If you mixed with the theatre crowd, and were not out with the lads, drinking, and attending football matches, conclusions were drawn, no matter how wrongly or cruelly they came across. But then, if Neil was not bothered about chasing the girls, he did not seem unduly concerned about countering other people's perceptions of him. He was never one for making a song and dance about things; he would cultivate his contacts, slowly and almost secretly, and present things as a *fait accompli*, giving the impression that things had happened overnight, when in fact he would have been working away on them for ages. If he saw someone who might be able to do him some good one day, or vice versa, he would make the necessary approach. Good at landing deals with the minimum of fuss, it was no doubt through just such connections that he managed to get Dust its Radio Newcastle airplay. No other groups had been involved.

His first position was as British editor of *Marvel* Comics, for whom he would translate the American slang into English, and draw 'bikinis on scantily clad women if they were considered too daring'.

'The first interview I did was with Marc Bolan for *Marvel* magazines when I worked there. It'd been pouring with rain and I was drenched; then, when I put the tape recorder on, we went and sat down on the other side of the room. There was a pause in the conversation and Marc just got up, went and picked up the tape recorder and put it down between us. I was dead embarrassed. He gave me a copy of his *Futuristic Dragon* LP but I was too cool to ask him to sign it, "To Neil From Marc Bolan". That would have been really fab. It's the biggest regret of my life,' remembers Neil.

From 1977, Tennant was to spend five years with MacDonald Educational Publishing, where he was responsible for a top-selling series of books on home decorating and cooking, amongst other subjects. The series was entitled 'The Dairy Book of Home Management'. He recalls, 'When I used to proof recipes, I'd think, "This sounds quite good". At lunchtime I would run home and make the dish.'

During his time with the company, the National Union of Journalists chapel become embroiled in a dispute over redundancies when they were all sacked, and as a result staged a sit-in which lasted four months. Sleeping in the office on a rota basis, Neil found himself one of the negotiators and on one occasion came face to face with Robert Maxwell, the publishing magnate who eventually bought the company. The dispute was settled and the staff reinstated.

In 1981 he switched to ITV Books, before joining the pop magazine *Smash Hits*, in June of the following year, where he could concentrate more fully on music. Even if he wasn't actively playing, he was interviewing those who were.

Two

A Lowe Profile

Christopher Sean Lowe was born on 4 October 1959, to Clifford, an accomplished jazz trombonist, and Vivien Lowe of 38 Napier Avenue, South Shore, Blackpool, Lancashire. A happy child, his cheerfulness extended to the playroom during his first years at school. At Thames Road Junior he became fond of sports and was appointed a house captain. Unfortunately, his feats on the athletic field did not extend to the blackboard, and he failed his eleven-plus. It seemed that he was destined for the local secondary modern, following many of his schoolmates, when his parents stepped in. They had bigger and better plans for their son, and as a result Chris took extrance exams for Rossall, a public school. But having passed the exam, the fees proved too expensive, so instead he took exams for Arnold School, which he passed and then joined.

Chris felt he was duty bound to work hard, as his parents were paying for his education, and by the age of eleven he had decided on a career – architecture. An odd choice at such an early age, it was probably prompted, he says, by the fact that the family lived almost a peripatetic lifestyle, moving from one home to another. As the studious side of him took over, he was opting out of sports and burying himself more in his books by senior school, and he never had a problem motivating himself to complete his homework. He had few cares in the world, except for the usual teenage problem – spots. He would agonize over them until a course of antibiotics cleared the way for him to hold his head up high again.

From an early age Chris was interested in music, no doubt gaining his early inspiration and education from his grandfather, a trombonist who was a member of the Nitwits, an oldtime, comedy–jazz act that worked in such cities as Las Vegas. Chris once saw them perform at the Lido in Paris but, as he said, 'All I remember are topless dancing girls with big hats'. He joined the school's Combined Cadet Force, in which he banged the side drum. His musical interests extended to the piano and trombone; he played the latter in the school orchestra. He and half a dozen friends would play at various functions, including weddings, anniversaries and birthday parties. He was also involved at the other end of the musical spectrum, playing in a rock group called Stallion. Practice was the order of the day, and Chris played only one live session with them, at a youth club.

Like Neil Tennant, Chris was something of a clothes pundit; as he recalls, 'I always tried to wear the latest fashions. I can remember wearing flares with buckles on the back, a Ben Sherman shirt with a button-down collar, and a tie.'

During his teens, he featured in a jazz/dance group known as One Under Eight, which actually consisted of only seven performers who also played with him at school. As members of the Musicians' Union, the combo played at various professional venues in Blackpool, and at formal dances, and were paid accordingly. Their repertoire consisted of Frank Sinatra songs and other standards of the day.

At home, Chris would sit at the piano in the dining room and let his imagination take control, pretending that great composers were writing through him.

Oddly enough, Chris was a boy who was centre stage in various groups, and had been a house captain at junior school, yet who confesses to never having wanted to stand out as an individual. He has always wanted to be a part of the crowd. He was undeniably fashionable, but only to the extent of what was being worn by his peers. He was never more outrageous than his friends. Unlike Neil Tennant, Chris would not dye his hair to make a statement about punk or anything else. He only liked to be noticed as part of the mass.

His interest in architecture had stayed with him throughout his school years, and in 1978 he went to Liverpool University on a five-year degree course in the subject. He says, 'I had only one dream. I wanted to be an architect. As a kid, for fun, I used to design houses for my family to live in. At university I realized that you can't be as creative as you'd like, and I lost interest in the profession. When I passed my exam, I decided to become a Pet Shop Boy instead of an architect.'

Taking his musical interests with him, Chris joined the orchestra, but lasted only a term. He had not enjoyed it, and music took a back seat as his studies progressed, although he did volunteer with a friend to work as an extra in *Carmen*, performed by the English National Opera at the Liverpool Empire. They played the toreadors.

As part of his training, Chris moved to London to gain work experience with Michael Auckett Associates, whose offices are on Chelsea Embankment. Gaining practical experience, he designed a staircase in an industrial development in Milton Keynes. When visiting it in 1988, he said, 'It's not a remarkable staircase, it's just a functional staircase.' He initially lived in with his parents' godparents in the suburbs, until he replied to an advertisement for a bedsit in Sydney Street. He was living a meagre existence, with little money. Having never liked to be on his own, Chris started making friends.

'We see him every now and again but he tends to keep this side of his life quite separate from his public side,' says John Hardie, the clerical officer at Liverpool University. Chris took a three-tiered degree course, but to this day is not a qualified architect because he never sat his finals. Out of the three degrees, he only sat parts one and two, gaining passes in both. As the course was due to be completed, 'West End Girls', the duo's debut single, was released. 'He thought that money was more important than being a poor, hard-up, architect! He still has every right to come back and take his finals,' says John Hardie.

On 19 August 1981, partway through his work experience, Chris quite by chance bumped into Neil Tennant browsing in a music instrument shop in the trendy Kings Road. They quickly identified with each other and struck up a conversation about the merits of musicians and synthesizers and, according to Chris: 'Our musical tastes were so different we decided to put them together and see if we could come up with something new. It started as a hobby really – it was all a bit of fun.' Their tastes were certainly diverse, with Neil into wordsmiths like Elvis Costello, and Chris into Imagination.

They discovered that they had a mutual passion for hi-NRG, hip-hop, Euro-disco sounds, a favourite of the Italian-American community and, in particular, Bobby 'O' Orlando, the New York-based producer.

By this time Chris had grown bored with his work experience routine. He admits to sleeping at his drawing board and partying all night at the Camden Palace. He and Neil eventually went their separate ways, but vowed to keep in touch. Chris returned to Liverpool and when his course was finished he shunned work, signing on the dole instead and crashing with a friend in London. He continued to meet with Neil, when they worked on their fountain of musical ideas in a small recording studio in Camden Town, or at Neil's Chelsea flat, on his synthesizer.

'Every time we went in, we would always write a song so we had a huge backlog,' recalls Neil. 'We did it because we enjoyed doing it. I don't think we ever really thought that we would get anywhere.' Chris found himself motivated by Neil's enthusiasm, although there was never talk about the two of them forming a group. They enjoyed putting down ideas as Chris fiddled about on the keyboards, and whatever they came up with they'd sometimes play to friends. Never harbouring thoughts of stardom, they were merely pleasing themselves, even though Neil was keen to further the musical relationship and had in fact taken things slightly more seriously in the same year that they met.

During 1981, he had been into a South London studio to lay down some of his ideas. At this time punk was very much in vogue, and it was hardly surprising that Neil's writing took its influences from this. He had been keen to record his own material ever since he followed up an advertisement for an audition in the pop newspaper *Melody Maker*. Sitting in a bedsit in Clapham, South London, it was suggested to Neil that he should form his own group. In the presence of his brother Simon, girlfriend Sarah, and accompanying himself on guitar, Neil recorded 'The Taxi Driver', 'The Man on the Television' and 'She's So Eclectic'.

As more songs flowed and matured, so too the Boys became more impressed with their respective abilities. In fact, one of the numbers they wrote at this time, called 'I Can't Say Goodnight', crops up on the Liza Minnelli album *Results*, which the Boys produced in 1989. Far removed from another of their favourites called 'Bubadubadubadubadum'!

Neil's lyrics were often quite obscure, much to the chagrin of Chris, who thought they should be straightforward. Sometimes they would involve themselves in a correspondence course, whereby Chris would give Neil a cassette of music he had written whilst in the North West, and Neil would for his part write the lyrics.

A year went by before Neil, who was working for *Smash Hits* at this time, called up Chris in Liverpool with the idea that they should put some of their musical thoughts down in the form of a proper demo tape. Digging into his pocket, Neil scoured *Melody Maker* for a studio on the cheap and discovered one at £6 an hour. Arms weighed down with Chris's trombone, Neil's synthesizer and Casiotone, they entered the studio, where they made better use of a synthesizer and piano. On tape went 'Bubadubadubadubadum', 'Oh Dear' and 'Jealousy', the latter written 'by post'.

They had the songs. They needed a name. They chose West End for no other reason than that they enjoyed walking the streets of that part of London. They would return to the studio at weekends, learning, and improving the material. Chris's parents and grandfather had been keen for him to follow a career in music, even while he was studying architecture, certainly an unusual parental ambition.

A song called 'Passion' by the Flirts struck the right chord with Chris, who got Neil over to his flat to listen to it. The song had been written and produced by the highly acclaimed New Yorker Bobby Orlando, known as 'Bobby O'. The Bobby O influence had struck and stuck. 'We were convinced he was a genius,' said Chris. It was then that fate played an important hand for the duo.

Three

The Bobby O Story

In 1983, Neil Tennant landed an assignment with *Smash Hits* to travel to New York to review The Police live in concert and to interview superstar Sting, who had also attended St Cuthbert's School. 'He's three years older than me, so I can't really remember him too well at school, although I have an old sports team photo and there on the end, looking rather more fashion conscious than the rest, is one Gordon Sumner, before he became Sting,' recalls Neil. 'When I met him [in 1983], he had an old school friend with him and the three of us were in the bar at Shea Stadium reminiscing about school. If anything, he seemed to hate it even more than I did.'

As far as Neil, the journalist-cum-musician was concerned, the trip to America provided a golden opportunity to create contacts. He was well versed in the work of New York-based, hi-NRG disco producer Bobby Orlando, and he was one of Neil's prime targets.

Bobby Orlando had by this time built up a very extensive background in hi-NRG, dance-oriented music. Well on his way as a recognized producer, he had had a lot of disco-type hits which had done well in the American music industry magazine, *Billboard*, and sold well through Europe; he had received three gold records by the time the female impersonator Divine, was to use his production expertise in 1980.

Divine was already an accomplished artist and had been in numerous cult movies. Running a small but successful record company, Bobby saw the opportunity of working with Divine as yet another opportunity to boost his growing reputation.

Viewing a partnership with Divine as a cute little gimmick, he agreed to take on the artist, at the time thinking it was going to be like a disco Amanda Lear, who was huge in Europe. The reaction from the public was immediate and tremendous, with big hits following. Despite this new-found success, Bobby's relationship with Divine was not as it might have been, with little warmth emanating between the two, although it was to prove a useful working relationship.

Divine's manager, Bernard Jay, was different again and he and Bobby got on far better together. According to Bobby, the success of Divine's whole musical career can be attributed to Jay, being Divine's right-hand man, best friend and manager. Says Bobby, 'My own relationship with Bernard Jay had its stormy moments over the years, but it was also very good, so because of that relationship the Divine thing worked out well.' Bobby was responsible for producing all of Divine's hits up until the time the singer signed to Pete Waterman, of Stock Aitken & Waterman fame, who subsequently has had monster hits with artists like Jason Donovan and Kylie Minogue. Not long after signing, Divine's health began a downward spiral that ended with his death two years ago.

Bobby Orlando's company, Nunzio Brocheno Productions, was also producing the Flirts, Lisa Lisa and the Cult Jam, and Full Force, as well as ancillary artists like Man to Man, who became big cult disco artists in England. The company's offshoot, Bobcat Records, was responsible for the release of a wealth of material in the early Eighties. At the company's peak, hundreds of records were released a year, selling 3000 to 4000 copies each, mostly hi-NRG disco destined for the underground market. That was the style so loved by the Pet Shop Boys, and Neil in particular. The music catered to a certain core audience, no matter what the label put out. The company was the forerunner at the time in this particular musical style and as a result had cornered the market. As the market was later to change, so too Nunzio Brocheno Productions and Bobcat Records moved into other areas.

A child of the mid to late Seventies, Bobby Orlando would be one of the thousands of budding musicians who would practise playing guitar for hours on end in their bedrooms. Closet guitarists copying lick after lick off the records of their heroes. 'If you were a guitar player you had to play guitar and therefore you had to practise. You had to be good. You had to really want it. You couldn't fake it . . . there were no samplers in those days,' says Bobby.

Then sampling came along. Although he feels that new computer technology took away true musicality, Bobby's company saw the potential immediately and was one of the first to introduce it to vinyl. 'Now any kid from the ghetto or the suburbs can go out and buy a sampler for five hundred dollars, a drum machine for three hundred dollars and he can make great records, whereas in the Seventies and early to mid-Eighties, if you wanted to make a record you had to be somewhat musically adept. So anybody in the world, your sister, my brother, could go and make a record today just by sampling.

'Unlike the past, there are no special skills required to make records any more, and this will ultimately hurt, not help, the music industry. I'm not putting down sampling, it has its place, but what you see now is that people are not sampling, they are literally lifting things – entire sections of records.

'I've got kids who walk into my office with records they have made at home that sound so good I'm amazed, but when we were making records before sampling, it would take hours to get that drum sound. Nowadays you press the button and you've got it.

'I really started losing interest at that point, and consequently from a business point of view, thank God I did, because everybody was losing their arse. Nobody but the majors is making money in the record business any more. Nowadays you have artists who sell ten million records or they sell nothing. When we were coming up, I would say to a group, "Oh, this is great, you've sold 75,000 albums". That was like a great sale. You made money. There is no such thing as that any more. Nobody has a following any more.'

The Pet Shop Boys were swept into the sampler arena, where a plethora of different sounds gave them the scope to experiment in order to achieve their idiosyncratic sound and style.

Bobby came up during the glitter and punk generation when crowds would wait in line at a pub or at a bar to hear the Sex Pistols or the New York Dolls. 'That doesn't happen any more. Kids today are the stars themselves. The audience has become their own star. That's what went wrong with music in the past five or six years. Not that there isn't some good, creative music out there. Maybe I'm just getting older but I really don't get that rush like I used to get when I hear a great new group. The first time I ever heard *ABBA* I almost fainted, they were just so wonderful.

'They were so poppy and sounded so clean. Likewise, the first time I heard the New York Dolls I had that same feeling, as diametrically opposite as they were. I don't have that feeling. I listen to MC Hammer, it sounds really good, I like it, but it doesn't move me. I can't imagine it can move anybody other than the fact that it's a great record, but it doesn't move you. Sinead O'Connor doesn't move me. That's not moving, it's just basic stuff.'

Orlando is quick to point out that some of the golden-oldie music is almost tacky. He places great music, great packaging, in the hands of groups like the Boomtown Rats, and particularly their first album. The kind of music that stirred you enough to want to be a part of it. As he says, quite rightly, there are no groups like that any more. He grew up during the particular culture that saw groups like Sparks and artists like David Essex in the charts, and thrived on it. Now, he says, it has all gone. Everybody is too rich today. Everybody has money managers, and if you need someone to manage your money, then you don't deserve to have that money. 'I reckon one of the reasons why the Pet Shop Boys are so elusive in some of their things is because they themselves might be caught up now in this whole idea of stardom, or whatever you want to call it.

'The kids coming up today, there is no reason for them to learn how to play because they are not going to sit in their room and play for hours until they learn how to play like we did. They don't have the discipline. There's no reason for them to sit in a studio for hours on end trying to get a particular sound, when they can just press a button. I'm not saying there is anything wrong with that technology, it is just that everybody's record sounds like the next guy's record. Nothing sounds unique any more. What's worse is that nobody seems to care.

'One good thing about some of these rap records that I am hearing now, though, is that while they have the sampler, there is a lot of live bass in there again, like the old James Brown, Joe Tex stuff, which I think is great. It's the bass that makes the hit.'

Bobby Orlando, the man with his finger on the pulse of everything that was hi-NRG disco, believes there is nothing outstanding today, whereas there was during the disco era. Donna Summer's 'Love to Love You Baby', with its sequential rhythms and hard, cold, Kraftwerk-type mechanical playing style, in itself so very Germanic, is a classic example of the type of song that Bobby will wax lyrical about. 'Nowadays, every record you hear sounds like that with sweetening on top of it, and as a result you have the likes of Jimmy Somerville, Erasure and Depeche Mode all sounding the same. Nowadays you have three or four different styles of music and everything within those styles sounds the same. Nothing is standing out any more,' says Bobby.

'Apart from the poseurs who stand on stage, press a computer button and do little else, the only style where people do still play is heavy metal, and you have to like heavy metal, which I hate! It's cult music today. Heavy metal artists are incredibly irresponsible with some of the things they do and say on their records. Not that artists are supposed to be the caretakers of the world, but at the same time anybody who listens to heavy metal is probably going to be a young, rebellious kind of a kid, and heavy metal artists should never forget this. I remember when I was a kid and I would listen to Alice Cooper. If Alice Cooper said go hang yourself I probably would have gone and hanged myself because you become so intrigued with rock heroes. The pop artists aren't like that any more, which is probably why we have a sense of frustration. They are no longer heroes of the youth, but traitors of the youth.'

He perceives the idols of today, like New Kids on the Block, as being like modern-day Bay City Rollers. Even the latter, he says, retained a certain charm. They actually played instruments, whereas the former merely dance. A contemporary version of what has always been around, but a little more syrupy. 'If you listen to the Bay City Rollers' albums now, it's great pop music. At the time you probably thought a lot differently. If there was a group who was playing that kind of stuff today, we would consider them geniuses. Maybe in ten years' time we will listen to New Kids on the Block and say, what creative stuff. Who the hell knows where it is going to go?'

A musician first and foremost, Bobby can't understand an artist not playing, like he can't understand a producer who can't play. But at the end of the day you do what sells. That's the record business. 'Too many so-called producers just sit around the studio reading the paper, drinking coffee and yesing the artist to death,' he notes.

'Do you think these new generation of kids are going to buy MC Hammer records in ten years? No. Maybe I would buy a Jeff Beck album for ever and ever because I just love the way he plays because I play, and I understand how much practice it takes to play the way Beck does. Kids today. What are they going to say? "I love the way he presses the sampler!" It's going to get much worse, too, before it gets better. You are going to see these guys are going to go on stage with tapes only, which is fine if you are going to a discotheque. Who cares? But when these guys are playing Madison Square Garden with tapes, it's crazy.'

As a semi-professional musician, I distinctly remember the emergence of samplers, and group vans – ours included – driving around with Musicians' Union stickers declaring 'Keep Music Live'. Many musicians, like Bobby O, were disturbed by what they perceived as replacement musicians – drum machines for drummers, high-tech keyboards in place of rhythm and bass guitarists.

The general public is not concerned with machines replacing instruments – they neither know nor care whether samplers or studio musicians have been employed as part of today's music genre. In fact, the huge advances in keyboard technology have been beneficial to many musicians, like the Pet Shop Boys, enhancing their music and taking them from their initial limited scope to a full studio production. This technology allows lyrical and musical talent to exist where shortcomings in playing an actual instrument would normally have prevented it.

Groups like the German-based Tangerine Dream are past masters at breaking new frontiers in digital techniques. They have helped lead the way for the Pet Shop Boys and MC Hammers of this world to bring studio sounds to the general public.

It has been argued that such studio-based mastery takes away from the live element by being too clinical, too perfectionist in its notation. Musicians make mistakes; machines don't. Punch in the notes and you get a perfect refrain, but crowds like to see the slick mastery of their guitar, bass and drum heroes.

For outfits like Soft Cell, the Pet Shop Boys, and MC Hammer, this was never the issue. Digital advancement helped to bring otherwise closet-bound, frustrated talents into the open. They weren't deliberately out to 'replace' those who had mastered their chosen instruments; they were merely capitalizing on progress. And no one can really blame – or criticize – them for that.

Four

Carrot Cake and a Recording Deal

Neil Tennant had been a big fan of Bobby O's hi-NRG disco records and, alongside Chris, had accumulated a large collection of the many records he had produced. While at *Smash Hits*, Neil would claim back on his expenses the money he paid out for imports, which at that time cost around £5 each. Mind you, it was hard to keep up with the prolific release schedule of Bobcat Records.

When he travelled to New York on his Sting assignment, by chance – or as fate would have it – Bobby O's office was at 1776 Broadway, the same office as a company called FBI Booking Agency, which happened to be the agency of the Police. Neil came to interview Sting in the building on 19 August 1983 – two years to the day since the duo had their first meeting in the King's Road – and while there asked for an interview with his producer hero.

'I thought, well if I've got to go and see the Police play, I'm also going to have lunch with Bobby O,' said Neil.

Neil described himself as a writer for a British pop magazine, and he and Orlando hit it off immediately. At the Applejack Diner – a hamburger joint on Broadway which was to become one of their favourite hang-outs – over a cheeseburger and carrot cake, which Bobby O paid for, musical ideologies passed back and forth, and Bobby recalls: 'I saw him, I liked him, we spoke.'

It was towards the end of their conversation, and almost as an afterthought, that Neil mentioned that he also wrote songs. Bobby does not recall hearing any of Neil's tapes at this juncture, but as far as he was concerned it didn't matter. The accent and the fact that Neil looked right was enough to sway the balance in his favour.

'I said, "You have a British accent, that's good enough. I'll sign you. We'll make a record," ' recalls Bobby. Despite the fact that Bobby had heard none of Neil's material, he said it did not matter. 'I told him to go and get his partner; I would fly them to New York and we would cut a record.' Neil was obviously thrilled.

'Meeting Bobby O was an even bigger thrill than meeting Sting,' admitted Neil later. 'I have admired his production techniques – with people like the transvestite singer Divine, as well as on his own records – for a long time.'

Upon Neil's return to London, the *Smash Hits* team were delighted at his good fortune. Bobby O followed up their meeting with a telex to confirm that the flights to New York would be arranged, which they subsequently were, and a couple of weeks later Neil returned to New York with Chris Lowe in tow. Sessions were held at Unique Studios, Sugar Hill (the Sugar Hill Gang studio in New Jersey), and at Bobby's own place, to make the perfect Bobby O New York disco record. They recorded 'West End Girls', 'Opportunities (Let's Make Lots of Money)' and 'One More Chance'. Ironically, the first two songs recorded were the same ones released by EMI after the Boys' break with Bobby O.

It was, in fact, Bobby who played most of the instruments live in the studio. 'Chris was not really a very good keyboard player,' says Bobby. An accomplished musician himself, Bobby wanted to lay out the material quickly, so he took the reins. 'I played everything on "West End Girls", including the jazz riffs at the end. Chris played one chord and the bass line. The choir sound we re-sampled off other records we had done.' The B-side of the single was 'One More Chance'.

Says Neil, 'We learned a lot. Bobby works fantastically quickly – within an hour and a half we had recorded the basic tracks for three songs. He [Bobby O] has a very low boredom threshold, so he works fast to keep the excitement going.'

It was immediately apparent that the trio hit it off well, and soon became close friends. The Boys stayed for about a week at an apartment Bobby was keeping at 56th Street, while he himself stayed up in Westchester County.

'What really compelled me to record them, believe it or not, was this certain gut feeling I had,' says Bobby. 'Neil had that look of enthusiasm in his face, and enthusiasm is everything. If you have that, you are going to win. I knew he was hungry and wanted to have a record, and that's more important than talent. And as it turned out they were talented too, which just made it that much nicer.

'A lot of the stuff you listen to of the Pet Shop Boys, and material by other artists that our company was putting out at that time, is the same sound. But the Bobcat Records sound of that period was very definable, very electronic, very high-tech, melodic and European.'

By the time Bobby met Neil, he already had ten gold records, all from Europe, so the company was well and truly established in that musical vein. Of his first impressions of Neil, Bobby recalls, somewhat tongue-in-cheek,'I liked him instantly. What's not to like? The guy is coming in telling me that he has bought every record I ever made. I said, "Gee, I must have made about one hundred bucks off you in royalties already." He was pleasant, excited, nervous, all the things that make a person nice. You almost feel humbled by such people.

'When I met Chris, he came in and was like this kind of goofy kid who walked through the door. In America we have a cartoon called "Mr Peabody and Sherman", it was a very big cartoon when I was a kid growing up. Mr Peabody was this little dog and Sherman a little boy; Peabody was Sherman's dog, but Peabody was the boss, Sherman was the sidekick. Peabody used to have glasses and he was this little character – brilliant, intelligent, an intellect. Sherman was this goofy little kid who hung around the dog. It would always turn out at the end of the cartoon that Sherman, although he appeared to be goofy, was always the wise kid, and Peabody would always, ultimately be rescued by Sherman. Mr Peabody and Sherman looked and acted exactly like the Pet Shop Boys! Mr Peabody was Neil, Sherman was Chris. It was like the joke of the office, "Here's Mr Peabody and Sherman".'

There was no contract on the Boys' first trip to New York, all having been done in good faith. Instead, an agreement was prepared for their second visit. Basically, Bobby said he would record them and see how it turned out. It was very loose. Although it was done so quickly, everything fell into place as it went along.

With the recording out of the way, presentation was next on the list. How was Bobby going to sell the two Englishmen to the American market? Bobby did not perceive it as a problem. 'I thought they looked great,' he says. 'They were telling me that they wanted to have a Duran Duran look. I disagreed. I said, "This whole pretty-boy glamour thing is nice; it works, but in your case I think, instead of trying to buck it, I think you should look staid, you should look like guilty Catholics. That would be the perfect look. Look intellectual, and look guilty. The world will relate, because the world is guilty. Leave your glasses on. The cuteness will come through if it is packaged right. The last thing it should look like is an attempt to look like pretty boys." It just wasn't going to happen. It was better for it to look like what it was so that they would almost be more respected as higher thinkers.'

Neil gave Bobby the impression of being intellectual, but at the same time very hip – that he knew what was happening. At that time, of course, Bobby was very fashion conscious, very clean cut. 'I never looked at them in the sense other than that I felt that they had a particular look that would benefit them if they adhered to that look. I advised them continually to always be as radical as they could be in whatever they say publicly, always put the big guys down.' This proved somewhat ironic; despite the Boys' proclamations about not wanting to be on a major label, ultimately they sought one. Every artist must dream of being on a major label at some point. 'Any childhood fantasy you have of being the young upstart at an independent label quickly goes away when you finally get some success.'

Having said that, Bobby O was thrilled with the way the production of 'West End Girls' turned out. The idea was for it to be a rap record done in a British accent. The gimmicky Britishness was something that Bobby could play on. Before releasing and promoting the single on his own label, Bobby played it around for some of the majors. Every one turned it down, including EMI America who turned it down cold, saying that Neil sounded like Al Stewart. At this point, Bobby had become extremely fanatical about breaking the Pet Shop Boys. The more people turned the single down, the more he was convinced it was going to be huge.

'If the majors hated it, then it had to be good,' he noted.

Although being basically disco, Bobby did not want to promote it as such, but as underground New Wave, as 'new music', which at the time meant nothing. As part of the promotion campaign, the company ran a free colour television giveaway. The question was, could anyone guess the name of the singer of the Pet Shop Boys? Sure enough, somebody in California won a free colour television.

The record was released in April 1984 on Bobcat, who also licensed it to Epic Records in the UK in a one-off deal. Bobby had been dealing through Gordon Charlton and his secretary Lorraine Trent at the company, both strong supporters of the Boys. Out eight weeks in America, it was doing well, picking up a nice buzz, particularly in the clubs in Los Angeles and San Francisco, when suddenly the whole campaign exploded. Bobby had gone overboard on promotion and it worked far better than expected. The record began to catch on and orders started pouring into Bobcat Records. Interviews with Neil and Chris were being demanded by punk-type magazines – and the big break was just around the corner.

'West End Girls', after receiving plenty of air and club play, was getting itself an underground core audience. WLIR, a new music station in New York at the time, since renamed WDRE, played it continuously. The record grew big the old-fashioned way, starting with a small audience and building up a large one. It was brewing all the time.

And it was decision time for Neil and Chris. Their careers were on the line. Neil, though, had some qualms: 'It was a risk leaving a successful magazine for music, but it was something I always wanted to do.'

Neil would lie awake at night thinking he must be mad leaving his secure job for something as fickle as being a pop star. Deep down he knew he was doing the right thing, and later admitted: 'I don't miss it. I liked meeting people but I didn't enjoy the writing. The only thing I miss is the free records. I used to get thousands of review copies.'

Nearing the end of his five-year architecture course, with his finals around the corner, Chris was anxious as he considered his future, 'My mum always told me I had to finish my exams, but if the song's a hit, I don't know if I'll make use of my training.'

The London-based paper, the *Evening Standard*, reported on 4 April 1984: 'A new duo, who go under the particularly silly name of the Pet Shop Boys, are waiting with baited breath to find out if their debut single is a success.'

The single went on to sell exceptionally well in France and Belgium: it had a far greater impact on the radio listeners of America's West Coast, but failed to move the British chart-buying public. Despite this obvious disappointment on home territory, it was enough to move the Boys to push ahead with another single.

High on their American success, Neil and Chris returned to New York to record more material; in fact, enough for three albums. According to Bobby, the material got better and better. Bobby would start playing, and Neil would begin to sing. Chris would join in, and the atmosphere created was reminiscent of a garage band. It all simply came together.

Neil says that at the time, despite their good fortune, they were quite happy to become a popular underground dance duo. Television, promotions and the package were not in sight or in mind, despite their first-ever stage appearance at the

Fridge in Brixton, London, in October 1984, when they sang and played over tapes. Making a record with Bobby O was their one and only goal. They wanted to be part of the Bobby O story.

Five

What's in a Name

There has been much talk over the years of where the name for the duo originated – and its gay connotations. According to the Boys, the name cropped up just prior to them recording with Bobby O. Chris had a flat in Ealing at the time, and he was acquainted with three boys who worked in a pet shop. The trio were already in a group, but it was nameless. Neil and Chris suggested they call themselves the Pet Shop Boys . . . 'We thought it sounded like an English rap group.' The Boys then ruminated over their own name, throwing ideas back and forth both in Britain and America, and finally latching on to their original idea for their friends. They have admitted since that they have been embarrassed by it, thinking it sounded silly and even camp.

But there were other problems, eagerly picked up on by the media. It was rumoured that 'pet shop boys' were gay American men who put hamsters (or gerbils) up their bottoms – for pleasure. Neil and Chris were obviously horrified when this was revealed to them after the release of 'West End Girls'. They even considered changing their name, but decided against it.

Bobby Orlando does not personally recall the Boys having chosen a name for themselves by the time they first arrived in New York. He says: 'I had an artist called the Beat Box Boys, with a song called "Einstein", an underground number which sold around 100,000 copies. The Boys and I were talking about a potential name. I said whatever it is, let's use a name like Beat Box Boys. I said, "Why don't you call yourselves the Altar Boys?", because I was focussing in on this staid Catholic image. They didn't like that and in retrospect I don't blame them. We were throwing names back and forth and the name Pet Shop Boys came up. [This was a name Neil and Chris had previously decided on. The rough mixes of the first day's recording carry the label Pet Shop Boys.] It didn't have any particular meaning. They certainly never told me that it was something based upon a friend who had a pet shop.

'Chris had said something once that there was some kind of meaning to the name Pet Shop Boys. Some kind of a culture, but I said it sounded fine to me. The name came around on the day we signed the contract. I said I could always change it later if they changed their minds. There had been numerous phone conversations with Neil after the first batch of sessions where we were throwing names around like crazy.'

Bobby said he had also heard the rumour about the gay subculture activities in New York, but no one had ever substantiated it, and the Boys' behaviour refuted it.

On the Boys' second trip back to New York, they travelled with Kimberley Leston from *Smash Hits*, who later moved to *The Face* magazine, and they stayed in a wonderful rented townhouse on the west side of New York. *Smash Hits* was setting up a magazine in the States called *Star Hits*, and Neil and Kimberley travelled to New York to ensure that the operation got rolling.

Bobby, Neil and Chris would often eat out at different restaurants and, at that time, as Bobby is the first to admit, he could not resist a pretty face. On one occasion a gorgeous girl walked into a diner and Bobby said to her: 'Do you know who these guys are?' He then pointed to Neil and said he was the lead singer with Duran Duran. The girl freaked out, saying she had all their records, and the Boys played it up to perfection. Although they would get a kick out of Bobby's spontaneity and play-acting, he found them particularly shy people, and certainly not as outgoing in the company of strangers.

They usually ate in the Applejack Diner, where Bobby knew the Greek owners well. Even before the Boys had a record out Bobby would insist that Neil and Chris should eat free there because they were the biggest group in England. The Greek owners of Café 57, an up-market restaurant, would fall for the same Bobby patter, rolling out the red carpet whenever the Boys were in town.

'Neil and Chris were as clean as whistles. They would stay at the apartment and they were *spotlessly* clean. They were not like typical rock-star animals in any way. There were a lot of big artists at that time that wanted me to produce them, and I turned every one down, mainly because I didn't think I could make enough money doing it. I thought: if I produce a group on my own label, I make a dollar; if I produce a group for another label, I make twenty cents. I burn out a piece of my talent and my own artists can say, "Why didn't you produce that for me?" So I always shied away from that, and I think Neil got a kick out of it because he used to think it was being kind of arrogant, which he liked.

'I think that leads into the way they are today – when you say aloof. As well they should be. I think it is funny when artists take themselves seriously. When they talk about their lyrics as if they were the Bible. What is it? It's not some great song. It's got a catchy melody, you're going to make a few bucks and you're going to go home. What's the big deal? But some people take their work so seriously. That's another thing I liked about the Pet Shop Boys and one of the reasons why I liked working with them – they knew all along that really it's all bullshit. It's just a question of, "We're going to have some fun, we'll make some money, and the more you can soak out of it, great." There was a certain charm to that. I think that they're right. It's almost the Malcolm MacLaren [who managed the Sex Pistols] thing. Grab the money and run. With some people I find that to be an exciting concept because it is bullshit anarchy; it doesn't mean anything. It's not like overthrowing the country or anything. It caters to a certain ilk of society. It's a revolutionary think. A phoney banana republic.'

*

Plans were drawn up for the release of the duo's first album when Bobby heard through the grapevine that the Boys wanted to switch to a major label. Bobby had been busily negotiating with CBS Records for the debut album. 'They said all the songs were weird. They wanted me to give them the real disco *cha-cha* record that I had become pseudo-famous for,' says Bobby. 'I said I thought they were wrong. At the same time the guys from Dead or Alive wanted me to produce them and I'd said no, for two reasons. One was because I was working with Neil and Chris, and I didn't want there to be any kind of conflict – because Dead or Alive was on CBS, and I didn't want a situation where I would drop one for the other, so I really protected my relationship with Neil and Chris by doing that. Also, I felt that the kid who was singing with Dead or Alive was in the vein of Divine, so I said forget it. As it turned out, Pete Waterman produced the single instead of me. Ironically, at that very same time Divine left Bobcat and went to work for Waterman also.'

Having tasted success with 'West End Girls', the Boys were obviously thinking big. They wanted to join the pop jamboree. Something was afoot, of that Bobby had no doubt, but there was no hint of their inner feelings the last time he saw them; he was busy planning their next moves. The Boys had been happy to be guided by his knowledge, by his professionalism, even to the extent that they allowed him to choose their first single. The Boys had wanted to release 'Opportunities' first, but Bobby did not think it as good a record as 'West End Girls'. Ironically, when the Boys later signed with Parlophone Records – a subsidiary of the giant EMI Records – in England, they contacted Bobby and told him that 'Opportunities' was being released as their first single. He told them it was a mistake. He said they should re-release 'West End Girls', as there was a whole bubble that had been created, which was still there to be taken advantage of. The Boys thought Bobby was wrong, and 'Opportunities' was released. It bombed. 'West End Girls' followed, and it was a smash hit.

'Opportunities' was borne of an original idea by Chris, who also came up with the title. Neil apparently wrote the words in about fifteen minutes. The song is anti-rock and anti-the-industry and its people. Although it sets out to destroy the credibility of the rock-pop music world, it was done as pure satire – a wind-up that was based on no one in particular, certainly not the Boys themselves.

As far as Bobby was aware, whilst on promotional tours of clubs and television stations through Europe, Neil and Chris had commented to various licensees that they would not be working with Bobby O any longer. The recipients of this news were clearly puzzled, as they had received no directive from New York to this effect. Bobby received a phone call from his licensee in Belgium, who had been awaiting the arrival of a batch of the Pet Shop Boys' debut album. Fobbing the rumour off with the reply that the Boys were no doubt just tired, Bobby immediately knew that there was going to be trouble. But he kept his cool and dealt with it in a professional manner. When he eventually spoke with Neil, the latter reluctantly agreed that it was true, that they had a commitment from EMI.

Bobby recalls, 'They came to me and basically they wanted to go with EMI, so I said we had two problems. One, I did not want to go with EMI, and two, I wanted to keep them on my own label.' This was a golden opportunity for Bobby to build on the foundations of Bobcat. That is why he had taken all the chances. Neil then mentioned the name of Tom Watkins, a manager in England.

Tom Watkins, like Chris Lowe, had designs on becoming an architect. Not having the necessary qualifications, he moved into interior design, before his thoughts turned to music. His earliest encounters were with the university circuit, where he organized package deals which included DJs and groups. It was during this time that he first came across Neil Tennant, who was engaged with *Marvel Comics*. Watkins had an idea to promote one of his bands, called Giggles, by using comic-book imagery, and contacted the *Marvel* offices, where he negotiated with Neil. The latter watched Giggles – who later worked with Sheena Easton – perform on several occasions, but at that time he was more into punk than pop music.

With several friends, Watkins formed XL Design, a company involved in record-sleeve design and concert posters. XL Design did work for various major artists, and was to design the sleeve for the Pet Shop Boys' Epic Records single, 'West End Girls'.

Watkins had also switched his interests to management, forming an off-shoot of XL Design called Massive Management. After hearing a demo tape of the Boys' songs, which included 'It's a Sin', 'Opportunities' and 'West End Girls', he agreed to take them on to his books. It was not a smooth beginning. From the outset it was obvious that Neil and Chris were their own men. They knew precisely what they wanted from the deal, and arguments occurred over the contract with Massive. Twelve months later the contract was re-negotiated after XL Design went bankrupt and Watkins bought out the management company. There were also on-going rows over the Boys' image. Watkins had firm ideas about glamour. The Boys had firmer ideas about maintaining their bored personas. They won. If they had capitulated, we may well have had two Bros lookalikes on our screens.

'It became apparent that they just did not want to be on our label any more,' says Bobby. 'I was very disappointed, obviously, but I felt the better part of valour is to just do what is appropriate and do what is best for myself and the company as well. They wound up on EMI, which is tremendously ironic because EMI had turned the artists down a year earlier.'

Bobby then fought hard with EMI. 'I thought they were just a big company; they reminded me of a guy who had turned a girl down earlier, then when the girl has an affair with another guy, suddenly the first guy wants to have the girl back.' Following the success of 'West End Girls' on Bobcat Records, Arista and Geffen Records had also shown interest in the Pet Shop Boys, Geffen also having previously turned them down.

'Someone had been talking to EMI – whether it was the Boys or Tom Watkins, I don't know – because all of a sudden, why were they interested, just by hearing the record?' Apparently CBS only developed an interest in the song after discovering at a business lunch that somebody from EMI wanted it.

Six

The Million Dollar Man?

Neil Tennant later commented that he felt the Pet Shop Boys needed a manager because it had grown obvious that, despite how much they wanted to keep hold of the reins, they could not possibly do everything themselves. They needed to bring in a manager to sort out a major record deal on their behalf. He had presumed that Tom Watkins would deal directly with Bobby O on this issue, but Watkins obviously had other ideas up his sleeve. Apparently, too many rights were already tied up across in New York.

Bobby O had certainly got the rough end of the wedge. Having successfully launched the Boys with their first single, he was already well on the way to negotiating a deal with a major label when the Boys broke the news that they were signing with EMI.

As a result, an arrangement was worked out between EMI and Orlando which did not prevent the Pet Shop Boys from recording. He says there was no problem with the Boys at that time. They remained on friendly terms. 'I knew that they would wind up using all the stuff that I had recorded anyway. They had to because it was great stuff.' Their first three hits were all songs that Bobby O had recorded.

As far as Bobby was concerned, from a business point of view he was still involved with Neil and Chris, and began corresponding with EMI to this effect. Moreover, he was really concerned about them. He honestly wanted them to have that success. In a sense he stands by that today. He says, 'I told the magazine *Billboard* in an interview at the time that if the Pet Shop Boys go along the path that I advise them to go on, they would be as big as the Beatles. Which was, of course, an over-statement, but I was trying to say that they would be huge.

'I never lost interest in them. At the time that I started working with them I had lost interest in my other projects. I was a successful businessman and I really felt this incredible creative impulse, something that I was longing to recapture in a sense by working with them, because it was not the traditional *cha-cha* disco stuff that I had been doing.

'I felt like I was working with real people as opposed to these fictitious names and characters that we would continue to make up. What had happened, however, was that because they lived in England and I lived in New York, during the times that they were not in New York, our only mode of conversation was by telephone. So there were times when they would call the office and I was out of town, so when I came back I would call them, but that was maybe ten days later, so maybe they would take that to mean that I had lost interest in them.'

Neil and Chris stated that they had grown frustrated and felt that they had themselves an unworkable relationship with Bobby O. Neil claimed that when they first started recording, it was in a 24-track studio, but later this switched to an 8-track in his office, and they felt they were regressing. Bobby O, he claimed, was not only eccentric but was also saving money, and they began to doubt whether he still had any faith in them.

Says Bobby, 'I don't see how Neil could have made that comment, only because when we were together we spent literally twenty-four hours a day together. We would eat breakfast, lunch and dinner together; we would hang out together; we would go walking down Broadway and shopping together. We talked about life, women, politics. You name it, we talked about it. These activities are all-important in production, even though it does not involve recording. It is assimilating the personalities.'

Prior to the split, Bobby had got into a phase where he had become obsessed with the idea of minimalism. 'At this point sampling was becoming commonplace and I said, "Why not do something that is raw, at its roots?" In fact, there was one track I had done with them that was like David Edmunds crawling from the wreckage kind of a thing, but they hated guitars. I said to them that instead of doing these 24-track songs, everything separated on each track, let's try to create a new thing of using minimalism. I wanted to record directly into 2-track, everything live. What are they doing today? Everybody is recording directly off the computer into the Dat machine. So we were recording certain tracks on the 8-track set-up that we had in our office; but this was not a track recording like making a demo at home, this was a professional studio environment with the latest technology. Some of the greatest things we did were as a result of that. I really wanted to get to this thing where it was drums, bass, keyboard, voice, that's it. Almost like House music is today: minimal. I wanted to try a new approach. From Neil's point of view, maybe he viewed it that way, but I spent a lot of money. Remember, I'm an independent businessman; I'm not CBS and we had spent what I consider to be a decent amount of money. People don't spend money, let alone their time, if they don't believe in something.'

Neil told journalist Chris Heath, author of *Pet Shop Boys, Literally*, that everyone thought they should give up Bobby O. Neil claimed that they did not receive money from him, or for the original version of 'West End Girls'. Bobby O's settlement included all the royalties from the Bobcat version of 'West End Girls', plus those of 'One More Chance' and 'Pet Shop Boys', the two other tracks he owns. Bobby also negotiated an override royalty on each of the Boys' first three albums, with a ceiling of one million dollars. He had in fact earned this sum by midway through the life of *Actually*, paid to him by EMI.

Bobby was also involved in the writing of the two songs, 'One More Chance' and 'Two Divided by Zero', for which he is credited as co-author and earns fifty per cent of the writing royalties. Neil does admit that the producer warranted the money, as he had taken a chance with the Boys, where others may have decided otherwise.

When I mentioned the figure of a million dollars, Bobby O commented: 'I was a successful businessman long before I met Neil and Chris. Neil said he never thought he would be successful, and for this reason they agreed to the terms of the deal, never actually believing it would pay off. But I always believed they would be successful and I always expected to receive what we had agreed to. I guess I believed in their success more than they did.

'There was this period of time where Neil obviously got into this thing where he felt angered, or frustrated. After they left us, in some of the early interviews they really praised me in all respects. If they were going to pay me off it would have been a lot more than a million bucks!'

Following the split, the trio remained on good terms. Every time the Boys were in New York, they would see Bobby at his office, take in lunch, talk, and meet some of the new artists on his books. Acrimony did come later, around 1987 or 1988, although Bobby says he does not know the reason. I understand the acrimony during this time was created because of the Boys' claim that they had not – and to this day still have not – received all master tapes that were due to them under the settlements previously made with Bobby O.

He says he never harboured any bad vibes about them. He actually received one call from Neil around 1986, but he says it was not the same Neil he'd once known. He was very cold. Bobby told him he sounded different .

'I had been incredibly successful as a businessman and as a producer before meeting them. I had remained so at that point, and it was only in 1987 and 1988 when I decided I'd just had enough for the time being; I wanted to get a breather.

And it did get bad at some point. Frankly, I never really figured out why.

'The last time I spoke to them was when their new album [*Introspective*] came out and I'd basically told them during that conversation that I didn't like the album, that I thought it didn't live up to their true talents. I thought they were taking the wrong direction. They said they would have thought I would like the new album. I said, "I like what you guys are doing but I think the guys who produce you do mediocre work." They have not been properly produced since the last good production someone did with them, which was "Love Comes Quickly". Everything after that has been garbage. "You Are Always on My Mind" was also a good production. Outside of that it sounds so rinky-dinky. They should produce themselves.

'I could almost understand why they chose to produce Liza Minnelli, because she has this Bette Midler attraction about her. I could see them producing Cher, for instance. There just seems to be something particular about these diva-type ladies.

'I think that at some point they got frustrated, or maybe they just started getting too rich . . . When I let them go to EMI I really sensed that they wanted to go. I don't think you can really legislate people's behaviour. If you are with a woman, and she wants to go, you can kick and scream as much as you want to, but she is going to go anyway. So, at that point, I thought, I like them, let them go. They are going to be huge and they will remember me and then it will work out fine. If you read some of the articles when they first went to EMI after "West End Girls" was a hit, there was nothing but praise for Bobby O. Then I read a few articles many years after that where it's like they never said those things.

'One of the reasons why, in 1987, I decided that I was going to start phasing out of the music business a little bit and take some time to do these other endeavours was because I really became incredibly disturbed over the ingratitude of many of our artists and people that we worked with.

'I still have this link to my creative past, that you tend to thrive on the gratitude and appreciation of those you work with. I think everyone needs to feel appreciated. So even if you want to use the argument "Who cares what they say as long as you get paid?" that's true to an extent, but to another extent it's like, "Why shouldn't I just do it for myself? Why should I let them be a part of it?" So there comes a time when appreciation is really important. And I certainly have never got that, I don't think, from any artist that I have ever worked with. And I don't think it is just me. At the end of the day, the artists all believe, once they become successful, that somehow they can do it themselves, and it's, "What did you really do for me?" Out of all the artists I have worked with, only one has been with me for twelve years, and that's Screaming Tony Baxter. We had one hit, "Get up off that Thing" in England, which went to Number 14 in 1984.'

The hardest part of breaking a record is not having the hit, it's having that ground-swell, that grass-roots backing. 'What we did for the Pet Shop Boys was we rallied that grass-roots network but we never invaded,' said Bobby Orlando. 'I really could have been a total arsehole about it but I wasn't. I thought: better off, I have got the thing going. Even if I am not going to be EMI, if we let this thing delay too long, people will forget about it. It's there, it has happened already.'

Bobby admits that he tends to get a bit radical sometimes, and felt particularly disturbed by some of the people that were working with Neil and Chris. He thought the Boys were poorly advised, advised in a way that was not true to what the existing situation was. Whatever frustration they were feeling, whoever was advising them at the time, had portrayed his company as just a bunch of little guys.

He says there was a good propaganda campaign levelled against the company. 'We were not a small company in the respect that we could not afford to record the artist. We were a *sizeable* small company, so it wasn't as if we had to worry about having our phone turned off the next month. I think that that also added to the paranoia that the two guys'd had.'

When the whole charade was over, Bobby thought to himself that even when you do it right, and have played by all the rules, moral and otherwise, people break. He could not have done more for any artist than he did for the Pet Shop Boys; he could not have put more of himself into it. To him, none of it made sense; yet, at the same time he looked at his business. He was comfortable and happy, he was moving into other areas, so now was the time to make a big plus, as music had been changing at that time, too.

He had wanted to remain friends with the Boys, to see their success through. He had enjoyed dealing with Neil, who to him had always been the duo's spokesperson, although, as Bobby says, Chris was no 'shy little goofball. That's a smart kid.'

'Chris appears to be the kind of guy that nothing bothers him – everything is wonderful. It's a great thing to have. He's the kind of guy, I suspect, that if everything went wrong for them, would say, "What the hell", whereas Neil would be the kind of guy who would probably dwell upon it forever and build it up out of proportion in his mind. That's not to say that Neil was not intelligent – he is, and is also a serious kid, although he has got a good sense of humour.'

Bobby never saw Neil as being manipulative. If he was, he says, he was very good at it. He always saw him as being someone trying to create an incredible façade. 'It takes a long time to get through to him. When you do, he is really a very sensitive, decent guy. He assimilates, which is a very good quality to have.'

The reason the three met in the first place was because Bobby O had swayed them musically and he says: 'One of the only things I missed in not working with Neil and Chris after we had split up wasn't *working* with them, it was just *being* with them, because we did have a lot of fun together. Every topic of life you could think about we had talked about and we had different opinions in many of those instances. I think their whole Bobcat Records experience influenced them greatly.

'I think we took their virginity from them. When you make love to a girl for the first time, and she has never been made love to before, you have got her heart forever. Whether she hates you or not, she will always love you. She will remember you forever. But then you grow up. It doesn't mean you want to marry them. It just means you will remember them. They will never forget me, nor I them; that's for sure! It was a good relationship.'

Seven

Let's Make Lots of Money

Chris was the classic vinyl junkie, according to Bobby Orlando, whose company charged over the odds for records. The underground disco 12-inch units would cost around eight dollars each. 'We never even gave you a long version. "Three minutes, they'll buy it" was the company motto,' he says. One of the reasons that the company was so successful was because it was the only game in town. When all the majors rediscovered dance music, they began to re-introduce 12-inch singles, by which time Bobcat had a strong hold in the market place. Ironically, the company never had the same success in the States as it had achieved in Europe. It was always only the underground market on home territory. 'There was always something about us in America, where the public at large, whether as a result of our music, distribution, or it was just a vibe about what we did, we were never able to break here the way we did in Europe,' says Bobby.

'Similarly, the Pet Shop Boys are big in America, they sell a lot of records, but they are not popular to the extent they are in Europe, where they are much more known as figures, as individuals, as artists, as stars. In America I don't think people know who they are other than they know the name and they know the songs. Generally it's because an American audience is not as sophisticated as a European one. An American audience tends to go for what is obvious, like Michael Jackson, who gets up there and dances around. He's not a subliminal star; the Europeans are often attracted to such stars. Marc Bolan of T. Rex was huge in Europe. In

America he wasn't an obvious star like Paula Abdul who dances around and does soft drink commercials. American stardom is almost like the kind of thing that might be uncool in parts of Europe.'

Bobby is talking here about traditional European pop stars. And from an American perspective, the Pet Shop Boys are not obvious enough. Americans seem to prefer artists who are more overt, or even radical, not politically or musically, but just in their performance, their voice, their mannerisms. Former bands like the Bay City Rollers are a classic example of the European way, as, oddly enough, were Sparks. 'There are three thousand miles of America between New York and California, and in that three thousand miles there are a lot of cows, sheep and farmers, and to them Lynyrd Skynyrd is what it is all about,' says Bobby. 'They don't want to know about prissy boys from England.

'America is not the fashion capital of the world like New York is. You go fifty miles outside of New York and you are in a different world. People tend to think of America as being this ultra-hip place, it's not. America is stodgy, mostly un-hip and filled with farmers. I know Neil and Chris viewed America as this tremendous place, once they became familiar with the country as opposed to New York. I remember Chris saying in 1988 he was looking to move to Los Angeles, California, which is kind of New York-ish – it's hip, it's modern. But you never hear anyone say, "I want to move to Arkansas!" Neil had talked of moving to New York at one point.

'When I first met them, they had no intention of taking the piss out of the music industry. During the course of our working together I always encouraged them to believe that that was exactly what they should do. And I based that on my own knowledge that the music industry doesn't want you. They have rejected you. If people reject you, do you want to kiss their arse or do you want to piss on them?

'The lengths the Boys go towards being political remain on a personal level: while they are, their songs are not. What's political about "Opportunities (Let's Make Lots of Money)"? I think it's more about the question of wanting to make as much money as possible, like anybody else. It's pretty straightforward. It's a business proposition.

'As a producer I would be involved with anybody with whom I felt I could make money, and do something that would be creative. If I did do it again with the Pet Shop Boys, it would have to be under the same terms and conditions as I did it before, which would basically be that I would have to have total control of what took place in the studio, and I certainly wouldn't be making the kind of records they are making now. So if the direction that they want to go in is what they have been making, I would never work with them again because I think what they are making is garbage.

'If I ever recorded them again I would not use a single synthesizer or sampler on the production. I would record their voices in a series of different, live, natural surroundings – with animals groaning in the background, airplanes taking off and landing in the background, cab drivers honking their horns, and such. Then I would convert the "natural sounds" to beats and rhythms and mix them with Neil and Chris's voices. The result would be a cross between Iggy Pop and Billy Idol with a British flavour. If the Boys let me produce them in this manner, then I would record them again. Otherwise, I would never again work with them in the studio.

'If they wanted to make another record like an "It's a Sin", or "You Are Always on My Mind", then I think I am uniquely qualified to make those kind of records.

'If I had to have any kind of a relationship with the Pet Shop Boys today it would be a managerial relationship. I would tell them exactly what they should be doing. I would tell them exactly why they should stop doing what they are doing. I would do that in a sense of getting them to make themselves a little more accessible to world markets. When "It's a Sin" came out they could have used that as an advantage to preach whatever gospel they wanted to preach.

'Them producing Dusty Springfield was a gain to Dusty

Springfield. Not to Neil and Chris. Let's face it, she's a great artist, a great singer, and she only made the record because Neil and Chris said "We'll produce you". They had the name, so they did her a tremendous service by producing her. And I can imagine the reason Neil and Chris produced her is because they had this youthful affinity towards her, probably the same that they had towards me when they first met me ... what compelled them to come and search me out. Likewise, Liza Minnelli. That was more personal pleasure that they derived out of doing that than anything else, because it did not benefit them more than it benefited Dusty or Liza.'

Eight

New Opportunities

Having signed a five-year management deal with Tom Watkins of Massive Management on 31 October 1984, Neil and Chris had to wait several months before their big break occurred in March 1985, when they organized a worldwide deal with Parlophone Records, who successfully fought off interest from several other major labels in order to sign them.

Neil left his position at *Smash Hits* on 5 April 1985. As a parting gift, the management presented him with a mock cover, displaying the headline: *'Why I Quit SMASH HITS To Be a Teen Sensation'*. The next issue predicted that 'in a matter of weeks Neil's pop duo, the Pet Shop Boys, will be down the dumper and he'll come crawling back on bended knees, ha ha ha.'

With the security of a contract firmly under their belts, the Boys headed straight for the studio to record the single 'Opportunities (Let's Make Lots of Money)' (back with 'In the Night'). As a pre-publicity gimmick, pictures began appearing in the Press, despite the fact that there was no product to speak of on the shelves. It was a clever ploy, and kept the general public bemused. That was until 1 July, when the single saw the light of day. It came in 7-inch and two different 12-inch versions. The first 12-inch was produced by Nicholas Froome and J.J. Jeczalik (producer for the Art of Noise). The second was produced by Ron Dean Miller of Nuance, and edited by the Latin Rascals, whom the Boys had met whilst in New York with Bobby O. Like 'West End Girls', it received plenty of airplay – including the Boys appearance on the TV show 'Poparound' – but failed to reach the nationally compiled Top Seventy-five, peaking at Number 116.

Despite the poor sales response, the single helped fuel the Boys' reputation. While promoting it around the club circuit in London, it dawned on Neil and Chris that 'West End Girls' was still a dance floor favourite – as Bobby O had intimated. As a result, and much against the wishes of both their record company and Massive Management, the song was re-recorded, this time under the production expertise of Stephen Hague, and taking about a week in the studio. It was subsequently released on 28 October, taking three months to break through into the Top Ten, where it went on to become the first Number One of 1986, holding the top spot for two weeks. It sold around 750,000 copies in the UK alone. 'West End Girls' eventually topped the charts in America, Canada, Finland, Hong Kong, Ireland, Israel, New Zealand and Norway, selling 1.5 million copies. It entered the Top Five of thirteen further countries. The association with producer Stephen Hague was firmly established. Neil commented at the time: 'People endlessly ask us what it's like having a Number One. But what it feels like is vaguely nothing. It feels like having a cup of tea.'

It had proved to be a case of better the second time round in England, as one of Neil's former colleagues was to write that the incorporation of street sounds created 'an atmosphere of danceteria sleaze that's almost sinister'. 'West End Girls' was not the first song to be given a successful second lease of life. The same thing happened with A-Ha's 'Take on Me'. It reached Number One only after a third national campaign by the group's record company. The same thing was to happen to Belouis Some, who first released his dance track 'Imagination' in 1985. It sold well in Europe and went to Number Two in Italy, but peaked at Number 47 in Britain. EMI re-released it and up it soared. 'I'm on the first rung of the ladder now and the world is open to me,' he reported. The world's oyster was definitely more open to the Pet Shop Boys.

Neil's local newspaper, the *Evening Chronicle*, reported, 'A new Geordie talent has taken the nation by storm – with a Number One smash hit record! "West End Girls", the first record release of new band the Pet Shop Boys, has reached the top spot in Britain's pop charts – and Gosforth-born Neil Tennant is reeling from the success. Now they are working hard recording their first album – due to be released in March – and Neil and partner Chris Lowe have barely had time to celebrate their Number One wonder . . . Now the Pet Shop Boys, already receiving sackfuls of fan mail, are all set to become the pop star heart throbs of 1986.'

Said Neil, 'The song was released in April 1984, but it did absolutely nothing in Britain. But we had great faith in the song. And when we signed with our new record company we decided to put out an entirely new version. Luckily for us this time round it worked.'

A spokesperson for Parlophone Records said, 'They were thrilled and amazed when they learned that "West End Girls" had got to the top of the charts. We all thought it had peaked when it got to Number Four at Christmas, so this is wonderful news. I think Chris and Neil took time off to drink a little champagne, but they are working flat out in the recording studio.'

Even flat out, Neil had time to make the following modest comment, 'It's a brilliant song, if I say so myself. It's completely original and doesn't sound like anything else. Everybody seems to like it, from DJs to mums and dads, so it must have something. I've sung it a hundred times and I'm not bored with it yet!'

The video of the single, for BBC-TV's 'Top of the Pops', was definitely a landmark in its stiltedness – especially to the Boys. Chris was seen hitting the keys on his board with only one finger, and Neil stood rooted to the spot wearing a drape coat. According to the Boys, they were merely repeating their performance in Belgium, when they thought at the time they were doing a radio interview, but instead they also had to perform. Chris merely played the bass line, which only required one finger anyway, and it accidentally translated into something that he felt was well suited to the actual mood of the song, it stuck. It was also an image that was to stick with the Press and public – sometimes in their throats.

Nine

Rudest Men in Rock

The change in fortunes came as quite a shock for the former journalist and his architecture-student partner. Suddenly they were the talk of the town and the darlings of the disco circuit. Says Neil, 'We were appearing at a special under-sixteens disco. All these millions of young girls started screaming our names and they even knew the intricate words to the rapping bit of our song. It was quite a shock.' The event also led to a reunion between Neil and George Michael, whom he first met in 1982. 'Meeting him three years later, I was happily surprised. He was as unpretentious as ever – unlike some pop stars I could mention.'

It took the Boys some time to appreciate that their sudden success had also been linked to the fact that the public liked their appearance. Never having thought of themselves as good looking, suddenly they and their names were in lights. Neil admits enjoying the thrill of adulation, of being at centre stage, although the Pet Shop Boys have never been seen to draw on pop's hysteria element. Even in their early publicity photographs they had not wanted to appear glamorous. They certainly did not want to look 'pretty' like Duran Duran or, heaven forbid, Culture Club. They wanted to look eerie, spooky, mysterious.

The pretentiousness of those early photographs was to continue – they would always refuse to smile at the camera, and Chris continued to say that people were given the wrong impression if ever you said 'cheese'.

Chris was desperate to grab hold of their change in fortune. The day 'West End Girls' reached Number One, he was attempting to stop his telephone from being cut off. He had just moved into a flat in London and the unpaid bill was for the connection charge. 'I thought at least they would have sent me a reminder,' he recalls. 'I got a call from a Mr Patel in accounts at British Telecom, saying, "If you haven't paid this bill by eleven a.m. we are going to cut you off." I didn't know anything about it – we had been celebrating on "Top of the Pops". I had to jump out of bed and rush to the Post Office.'

If the hoped-for fortune had not materialized, the sudden fame that normally goes hand in hand had not sunk in for Chris, who claims that it was his family and friends back home in Blackpool who were the most excited about his progress. 'It's strange because I think it means more to family and friends – they are more excited than I am. I wasn't as excited as I should have been. I don't think it's registered yet. But sometimes when I'm walking down the street I suddenly realize what's happening.'

No doubt Chris was reluctant to admit to his delight because he was not convinced at the time that the new version of 'West End Girls' would be such a success. 'Both of us liked it and we still do, but it doesn't necessarily mean it's going to be a hit. There were times when we were worried no one would play it on the radio, and without that there is no chance.'

The Boys turned down a fistful of dollars when an American soft drinks company asked permission to use the rapping part of the song in a television commercial. As Neil explained, 'They really offered a fortune, but it would cheapen the record.'

Chris had spent Christmas in Blackpool, where he heard 'West End Girls' being played in a disco – but nobody recognized him! He fostered that anonymity. 'I like to be anonymous. I disguise myself a bit to keep it that way,' he admitted. Even so, he was quite prepared for the Press and media attention, taking it all in his stride for someone so reluctant to step into the spotlight. 'You do so much of it, but I think it's worthwhile,' he told the *Evening Gazette*, in Blackpool.

'Pop music has never been about being a musician,' says Neil. 'It's just about having ideas. That's why videos are important. All you need is one idea. And as technology becomes simpler you can do it all yourself.'

Chris blames the first-time-round flop of 'West End Girls' on the fact that few radio disc jockeys played it over here. 'The trouble is there is not enough pop radio in Britain. In America, radio is much more exciting. The way they present things is sexier, more entertaining and faster. Over here, the music is broken up. Suddenly you get Steve Wright interviewing a Royal Navy commander on the Radio One Roadshow. Who needs that?' he noted.

Said Neil at the time, 'Sometimes I think maybe we strayed to the top by accident. To me it seems the charts aren't real at the moment and in a few weeks' time there will be a real chart with a proper group at the top and life will have returned to normal.'

The newly dubbed 'Rudest Men in Rock' felt that other groups took them too seriously – even the Radio One DJs. 'I heard that because we slagged off Radio One, a couple of DJs refused to play our records. It's so daft. I mean, those are exactly the people who would in the same breath slag off British Rail because they were delayed coming to work. We don't mind if people slag us off. There was this Belgian journalist who came to interview us and he started off by saying, "I think you're artistically barren." That was really good. We don't mind,' said Neil.

Two stars that the Boys did not savage at this time were Madonna and George Michael. 'They are both very single-minded and ambitious,' said Neil. 'When I met Madonna in New York she said she wanted to become the most famous film actress in the world and I'm sure she will. I've always liked George Michael because he is unpretentious and not obsessed with himself.'

*

The last week of January caught the Boys in Germany, where 'West End Girls' was lying at Number Three in the charts. Neil was happy to phone his parents three times a week while he was away, reporting on his activities. For his parents, Bill and Sheila, the radio alarm waking them with the sounds of their pop-star son was sweet music to their ears. They had never dreamt that their studious, history-loving eldest boy would make it big in the world of music. Bill said he could not imagine that the son who preferred reading a book to participating on the sports field, and was more than happy to remain in the background, could tour up front like his fellow school pupil Sting.

'At St Cuthbert's School, where the music tuition was excellent, he did take part in the Gilbert and Sullivan productions, but only in the chorus. He was never one of the leading lights,' said Bill.

If anything, Neil's success helped his parents appreciate pop music. 'Since his record got in the charts, we started listening to Radio One and watching "Top of the Pops". I really like Whitney Houston and the Bronski Beat. It has made me feel a lot younger,' said Bill.

Sitting pretty in the charts and supported by a growing army of fans, the last thing the Boys needed was the teenies reading what some claimed the name 'pet shop boys' meant. The pet-shop shocker was revealed on 3 February 1986 in the *Evening Standard*, which intimated that it was a term used by American gays. 'And anyone familiar with the, er, wilder side of New York nightlife will tell you that pet shop boys are not young men who work in pet shops. In fact they're gentlemen who derive satisfaction (or make money) from suffering pain. Whips, wellies and chains – that sort of thing.'

EMI, of which Parlophone is part, were horrified at the revelation. 'Oh God, you're not going to print that are you,' they squealed. 'The bosses here have been dreading something like this coming out ever since the boys got to Number One and Neil Tennant decided to tell them.'

Neil, though, had a different story to tell, as he pointed out in *Melody Maker*, 'One of the newspapers said that it's New York slang for rent boys who are into S&M, but if it is, it's news to me. We did genuinely call ourselves after some friends we had who worked in a pet shop in Ealing. We wanted something like that hip New York Peach Boys ring to it. If it has got that slightly dubious connotation then it's quite amusing but it's certainly not deliberate.'

Chris was happy to back his partner. 'It's funny but we've got a knack for managing to get ourselves into trouble without even trying to. We've got no intentions of being "subversive" or "dangerous" but we still always seem to be the ones who get tut-tutted at by EMI. It's never Sigue Sigue Sputnik. We never set out to do it.'

What they did was set out to make the perfect Bobby O New York disco record.

The Boys managed to avoid any probing questions as they hopped over to Europe on a promotional tour. Not that Neil was particularly happy to be stuck in Milan when he would rather have been working on their first album. 'This tour's just for promotional purposes but it's getting to be a bit of a pain because it's just holding everything up.'

Italian disco had played a major influential part in Neil and Chris's early writing, and it was one of their ambitions to be successful in that country, more so than most other European territories. 'If we wanted to be big in Italy we'd have to take the "whoooah" chants from something like the Baltimora record and put them on top of a disco beat,' explained Chris. 'We could also do something a bit deep and intense because that's very popular here as well. The Cure, Simple Minds, the Lotus Eaters, that sort of sensitive thing is appreciated. What we do is somewhere in between. Everyone would like it. Or maybe everyone would hate it.'

All did not go swimmingly on the Italian job. During one rehearsal for a television show that was to go out live, the Boys simply stood on stage and sang. When it came to the real thing, dancers came on stage and surrounded them, doing a most peculiar routine. According to Neil, the cameraman was more interested in the dancers, so he (Neil) turned his back. Chris had lost faith in the performance altogether, and gave up miming.

'A lot of things happen in Italy that don't happen in England. The photographers take pictures of you in front of a psychedelic screen because you are in a pop group, and you are expected to "do a different pose" all the time.' Apparently, the said photographers were particularly upset when Neil and Chris refused to smile. On one hand, you couldn't really blame them. On the other, it grew to be something they rarely did anyway.

The course of true love was not to run smoothly with photographers or, particularly, with the Press. Having been involved on both sides of the fence, Neil was not impressed with the media's attitude to either the Pet Shop Boys or pop music in general. 'When I started at *Smash Hits* the whole idea of daily papers being interested in pop personalities was inconceivable. There was no way the *Sun* would put Phil Oakey on their front page in 1982, but now there's no surprise at Simon Le Bon being there. It's all got so much more brutal now as well.

'All that stuff about our name meaning something seedy was surrounded by phrases like "Mums and dads buying records for their kids buy teeny sensation the Pet Shop Boys". For goodness sake, "mums and dads" never buy our records for their kids. These papers can only function by reducing life to the level of "Dynasty".'

Neil was somewhat naïve in pointing out that the Pet Shop Boys had never sought publicity. This is one of the very foundations on which the structuring of a pop career is based and cannot be dismissed so lightly. 'It's not the slightest bit difficult to set up a story, anyone can manipulate the media by being shocking. It's all a bit pointless.' Then again, does not notoriety breed success? The Rolling Stones are a classic example. Neil had a point when he said that the Pet Shop Boys were a bit amateurish to be proper stars, never having liked the ruthless professionalism of the industry – 'the sort of attitude when you get good at being on breakfast television. Actually, we were quite good on Breakfast TV! We haven't got that terrible glib approach that so many others seem to have and we're not going to get caught up in all that. Fortunately, we've got a few people around us who positively sneer at what we do!

'There does come a point when you realize that it would be very easy to go all out and become a pop star. That's when you have to stop and think, "No, that's not what I want to do." '

They certainly proved the point by remaining so aloof from the rest of the pop fraternity. They saw no reason to have to be polite in terms of talking to others simply because they were heralded under the pop umbrella. 'All that "loved your new single" when you thought it was horrible, rubbish, it's just a waste of time. I think we see ourselves differently. I mean, I always thought of us as having more in common with someone like Chakk than Duran Duran,' said Neil.

Ten

Paninaro Poseurs

A video produced by Big Features Ltd, and directed by Andy Morahan, was issued, helping to maintain the momentum, before Parlophone capitalized on the success of 'West End Girls' with the release on 24 February 1986 of 'Love Comes Quickly', produced by Stephen Hague and recorded at Advision Studios, with 'That's My Impression' on the flipside. The 12-inch version included 'Love Comes Quickly' (dance mix) and 'That's My Impression' (disco mix). The single reached a disappointing Number 19 in the charts the following month, yet helped establish the duo as one of the major acts of the year. Chris Lowe was featured in a half-obscure portrait pose on the picture sleeve – a design he had done in collaboration with Mark Farrow.

On 24 March their debut album, *Please*, hit the record shelves. It was somewhat of a tongue-in-cheek, but very clever, title, prompting politeness from fans, who would pop into their local store and ask, 'Can I have a copy of the Pet Shop Boys' new album, *Please*?'

One of the album's obvious main selling points was the inclusion of 'West End Girls', plus 'Love Comes Quickly' and the track 'Opportunities (Let's Make Lots of Money)'. As the *Evening Gazette*, Blackpool, observed: 'Tennant's voice is remarkably like folkster-turned-singer-songwriter Al Stewart, and the duo's style is firmly rooted in Euro-disco – but it is a combination which works remarkably well on the ten tracks here.

'Some of the ideas are pretty basic – tape cut-ups to start "Two Divided by Zero", New York "overdubs" and the occasional inclusion of a "name" such as former Roxy Music sax man Andy Mackay. Surprisingly, though, it all gels very well and little will stop it selling in droves and guaranteeing the duo success for at least the next few months.' It did, by reaching Number Three in the charts. By the end of the year it had gone platinum in the UK and America and become a fixture in the album charts of many other countries.

The themes concentrate on the realities of living in the modern world, and lean towards the emotional ('I Want a Lover' was, in fact, written from the point of view of a woman. As *Record Collector* correctly pointed out, it contributed to the sexual ambiguity played on by the duo), the strange and the sometimes blue, making it difficult, if not impossible, to tie the Boys down to any particular vein. The musical content yet again ripples with melancholia.

On 6 April, Jeremy Lewis wrote in the *Sunday Express*, 'EMI's pet pop duo, the Pet Shop Boys, have released an album called *Please* in the best wrap-around of the year. Normally a record company will spend only this much time and money on a sleeve if the record inside is bad. For they have to sell the stuff somehow! But this sleeve contains a winner. *Please* is a cross between nice, clean, suburban pop and the sort of thing you hear in the bars of dodgy Italian hotels. Great. It contains their two brilliant singles, "West End Girls" and "Love Comes Quickly". I think the Pet Shop Boys are as good as a pop band can be.'

Praise indeed.

Prior to the release of their follow-up single, 'Opportunities (Let's Make Lots of Money)', issued on 19 May, Neil announced to the *Daily Mirror*, and the world at large, about plans for their first UK tour. Reeling from the successes of 1986, he confided, 'It won't be the usual type of show. There will be lots of different things on stage and we will be playing theatres instead of concert halls. It will probably be so pretentious you won't believe it.'

No one did.

The tour plans for Europe and America were cancelled in June – the costs of a theatre, designer and appearances at fairly small venues proving prohibitive.

'Opportunities', re-mixed by Stephen Hague with help from David Jacobs, had, on the 12-inch version, overdubs supplied by Ron Dean Miller in New York, including the sounds of scaffolding falling, plus other special effects. The single came with 'Was That What it Was?' The 12-inch featured four tracks – an extended 'Opportunities', a reprise, the original dance mix (re-mixed by Shep Pettibone) and the regular 7-inch B side. Neil was concerned that his background may have worked against the duo in the initial stages, particularly as 'Opportunities' was not entirely seen in a favourable light by his former fellow music journalists. 'Opportunities' was meant to be funny – a pop group, just signed to a big record company, singing 'Let's Make Lots of Money'. But they all took it seriously. Sour grapes, perhaps.

The re-released single made it to Number 11, while across the Atlantic, 'West End Girls' soared to Number One.

'It's important to make records that people treasure. Loads of groups have no conception of that, they just put out far too many records, then nothing for a year and a half, by which time no one even cares. We're waiting for the right time, then putting something out that people will want to keep for ever,' said Neil prior to the album's release.

'It's like those stupid big centre labels we've had on the last two singles. They look brilliant. When we got the re-mixed "Opportunities" back with the big centre and the black sleeve, well, it's the sort of thing I'd always put at the front of my collection.'

By August 'Opportunities' was lying at Number Ten in the American charts and *Please* was at Number Seven. The Boys were a worldwide success and the mystique was building. They would rarely give interviews, giving next to nothing away, and arduous promotional tours gave way to videos.

Despite mounting pressure from the general public, the Press and their record company, the Boys refused to tour.

A new five-track EP was released on 22 September, helping to stall the disgruntled fans. In a limited edition of 25,000 copies, it consisted of two singles in a double-pack sleeve, with 'Suburbia Part 2' completing the EP. Promoted with the aid of a video produced by Eric Watson, it made Number Eight in the UK charts.

'Suburbia' was a new version from the *Please* album, and was produced by Julian Mendelsohn. The song was inspired by the Penelope Spheeris film of the same name, about a group of disenchanted, rebellious youths in suburban Los Angeles. Said the duo, 'It's about a riot happening in some decaying suburb. It's just the description of the riot happening and then the aftermath.' 'Paninaro' was inspired by the Italian Paninari youth cult, and featured Chris Lowe rapping for the first time. It was produced by the Boys and was issued in Italy as a single at the end of September.

The Boys were intrigued by the strange sub-culture in Milan known as the Paninaro, so-called after the Italian for 'sandwich', one of the paninaro's trademarks, donning Armani jeans, Timberland boots and US Air Force jackets with fur-lined hoods. 'The Pet Shop Boys would love to be the seminal paninaro band, usurping Duran Duran who, ludicrously, currently occupy that role. They are busy snapping up as much paninaro gear as possible, revelling quite rightly in the trivial obsessiveness of it all, and confounding their public,' stated Paul Mathur in *Melody Maker*.

'We played this TV show [in Milan] and I'd worn my long Stephen Linard coat. This boy came up to me in a club afterwards to say he really liked us and he was horrified that I was wearing my paninaro jacket! It just wasn't the done thing at all. He was a strange boy, though, he asked me if I knew the bass player out of Wire and was really taken aback when I said I didn't,' said Neil.

The third side of 'Suburbia' contained 'Love Comes Quickly', a Shep Pettibone remix. The legendary New York disc jockey spent so long re-mixing the track earlier in the year that it missed release. Now it was climbing the US charts and cropped up on the EP in this form for the first time. Side four contained 'Jack the Lad', a new song produced by the Boys, and 'Suburbia Part 2'.

A two-track single of 'Suburbia'/'Paninaro' was subsequently released, plus a 12-inch single of 'Suburbia (The Full Horror)', a nine-minute mix of both parts of the song, plus 'Paninaro' and 'Jack the Lad', and a cassette single of 'Suburbia (The Full Horror)', 'Paninaro', 'Love Comes Quickly' (the Shep Pettibone remix) and 'Jack the Lad' were simultaneously released. The Italian-only 12-inch of 'Paninaro' featured two versions of the track and came in a limited edition picture bag, released in November.

At the time of the 'Suburbia' release, the Pet Shop Boys were in Los Angeles appearing at the MTV Awards where they had been nominated for 'Best Performance of a New Group in a Video' for 'West End Girls'.

By October 'Love Comes Quickly' had stalled at Number 62 in the US charts. The following month, 17 November, saw six special 12-inch mixes of hits from *Please* repackaged as a UK mini-LP entitled *Disco*. It achieved sales of over 100,000 copies within the first six weeks and went on to reach Number 15 on the album charts. *Disco* had a running time in excess of forty-five minutes and featured 'In the Night', 'Suburbia', 'Opportunities', 'Paninaro', 'Love Comes Quickly' and 'West End Girls'. Arthur Baker, Julian Mendelsohn, Ron Dean Miller and the Latin Rascals, Shep Pettibone and the Pet Shop Boys all had a hand at the re-mix stage.

Says Neil: 'When we first came over to America, we actually pushed the idea that we were a disco group. We were trying to reclaim *Saturday Night Fever*. That's why we called our re-mix album *Disco*.

'The idea of a disco is, to me, a rather exciting idea. I guess it's an idea that's more exciting than the reality in some ways. You know the frenetic excitement, the sexiness of it, the lights, music, the lasers. It's an escapist idea, I suppose. Chris is the one with the major disco background.'

The latter's disco-mania was spawned from his days in Blackpool, which boasts a plethora of clubs and discos, mostly open the year round. 'I used to have jobs like glass collecting in Dixi-land Show Bar,' says Chris. I just liked the whole business. Before I started doing that, before *Saturday Night Fever*, there was nothing I really liked. I didn't like rock music. People used to listen to Alice Cooper, Uriah Heap, and things like that. I just thought it was absolute rubbish. It wasn't until *Saturday Night Fever* came along that I thought, "This is absolutely brilliant." It transformed my life.'

The successful year was rounded off with the release by Picture Music International of *Television*, a compilation video which included clips from the hit singles 'Opportunities', 'West End Girls', 'Love Comes Quickly' and 'Suburbia', plus a rarely seen video for the original 'Opportunities' single. There was also an exclusive video shot on location in Milan featuring 'Paninaro', never before seen in the UK. It was produced and directed by the Boys who also, naturally, starred in it. *Television* was linked with clips taken from various UK and foreign television shows as far afield as Italy, Australia, Germany, Japan and the States, including some fascinating interviews and performances, and appearances on 'Top of the Pops' and 'Soul Train'.

Despite Neil's dislike for compilation albums, the Boys' hit 'Suburbia' appeared on *Now That's What I Call Music 8*, which sold well in December.

As Christmas drew near, Neil and Chris were busy writing material for their follow-up album to *Please*, which, as well as going platinum, had spawned four hit singles. 1986 hadn't turned out to be a bad year at all.

Twelve months earlier, Chris and Neil had played to two thousand screaming kids at a junior disco in London. 'We haven't performed much before but that was really good,' Chris said at the time. 'I think I'll enjoy doing a tour.'

The world was holding its breath.

Eleven

They've Got it Taped

The New Year dawned with *Television* topping the UK music video chart, and the album *Disco* reaching Number 95 on the album charts in America. *Television* was a half-hour-long tape of some of the Pet Shop Boys' videos interwoven with a selection of their various worldwide television appearances. 'We didn't want to do just a compilation tape,' said Neil. 'And since we spend almost all our lives travelling around the world to star on TV programmes, we thought we ought to include some of it. Besides, we'd be terrible at doing those wacky links like Madness or somebody. I like the unreality of seeing yourself on TV in America or somewhere, so we shot the clips off a real TV to emphasize that. It doesn't even feel like me up there.'

The tape begins with the Boys appearing live on a Japanese television show which went out to 23 million viewers. They had planned to make their entrance down some steps, but completely messed it up. This semi-disaster is followed by 'Opportunities (Let's Make Lots of Money)', the first video from the Pet Shop Boys, which was directed by Eric Watson. The video in fact bears little resemblance to the song's story-line, but it still proved their most popular on MTV.

'West End Girls', admits Neil, was a cop out on everybody's part. 'We did something quite literal which we didn't want to do. Looking at it now though, I really like it. There're bits when it's sort of generally political, which works well being just a fleeting moment. I wore the same outfit as in "Opportunities" and Chris sort of hung around in the background. It's funny, in America they think all that hanging around's really cool for Chris to do. It's always him who they talk to first. They say, "How did you think of just hanging around?" '

The video for 'Love Comes Quickly' proved quite controversial, because Neil loved it and Chris hated it. Said Neil, 'I like the bit with Chris trapped on the grid but some people say that it's naff. I get really annoyed when people say that it's all contrived and calculated. Our songs sound painfully innocent to me. We're certainly not clever pop strategists or anything just because I was a journalist once. We've never had a strategy in our lives. The song was only ever a real hit in Spain.'

'Opportunities' was the video the Boys did for the re-mix, and was handled by Polish director Zbigniew Rybczynski, who was responsible for the Art of Noise video *Close to the Edit*. To him, it was a simple story of a capitalist and a worker, and the video carries the only shot of a guitar to appear in a Pet Shop Boys video, no doubt due to Chris' pet hate of the instrument.

'Video Soul' is an odd video. According to Neil, they were particularly tired for this shoot and hardly moved a muscle during the performance. At the time of 'Suburbia' Neil was hooked on Penelope Spheeris' film about punks in Los Angeles. The Boys have always striven to move away from the norm, and their videos prove it; this one in particular. There is an undercurrent of violence throughout, but as Neil qualified, 'I don't want us to make all our songs into a cartoon for children's television.'

They enjoyed doing 'Soul Train'. 'It's the thing you see when you watch clips of US TV when you're growing up,' said Neil. 'There's this presenter, Don Cornelius, who wouldn't let us do "Love Comes Quickly" because he didn't think it sounded like the Pet Shop Boys. We did "Opportunities" instead and he comes on telling us that it's really "funky".'

The Boys filmed the video for 'Paninaro' in Milan themselves for £9500. 'I think the video as a whole works really well but I don't think there'll be a *Television II*. It'd be a bit boring,' said Neil. 'We were originally going to have a kind of cut-out TV frame around the picture with knobs and everything but we ditched it. I would have liked to have had more of the TV shows.

'At the beginning it says "The Pet Shop Boys on Television", not "in". That's very important.'

Despite the success of *Television* and *Disco*, not everything was going exactly swingingly for the Boys. On 10 February Neil collected the Best Single award for 1986 from Boy George for 'West End Girls' at the British Record Industry Awards (BPI) at London's Grosvenor House Hotel. Chris decided to boycott the awards because he hated being judged, 'just like at school prize-givings'.

At a party afterwards hosted by Phonogram Records, the group Siouxsie and the Banshees attempted to gatecrash. Neil went across to the band, who had been refused entry. As other guests, including Mark Knopfler, Pepsi and Shirley, and Bob Geldof and his wife Paula Yates, carried on chatting and drinking, oblivious to what was happening close by, Neil attempted to persuade the bouncer on the door to let them in. Tempers flared and the bouncer threw a punch at him. Fortunately for Neil, he missed. Other security staff then quickly appeared and the scuffle spilled over into the hotel corridor.

Neil explained later: 'I find I can get carried away just as good on three cans of Red Stripe. I had a bit of a ruck at the BBC while filming "Top of the Pops" because of that stuff and I also had a brilliant argument with a bouncer at the BPI awards. I actually went up to this big guy to defend Siouxsie and the Banshees when they weren't going to let her in.'

Eventually, the band stormed off, but not before Siouxsie had grabbed Neil by the arm and yelled back: 'You can't do this to him, he's just won Best Pop Star or something. This isn't the record industry – it's the retard industry.'

A spokesperson for the record company said, 'The security people were told not to let anyone in without an invitation. It was only supposed to be a small drinks party. In the end the hotel had a go at us because there were too many people in the room. They had to be strict.'

A spokesperson for Grosvenor House said there had been an 'incident', but that no hotel security people had been involved. And Showsec Security, who were responsible for coverage of the awards ceremony itself, denied that their guards were involved. 'The record companies made their own arrangements,' they said.

The Boys had been busy working on their next album, and looking further into the possibility of touring. Neil was to comment, 'I can't see the point, really. I quite like the idea of being on the coach, having the meal beforehand, the party in the room afterwards, going in the swimming pool, signing the autographs in the lobby, wrecking the mini-bar . . . The only thing I don't like the idea of is being on stage and having to sing for rather a long time.'

This comment had been inspired by Neil's fond memories of joining Depeche Mode on tour, for an article in *Smash Hits* in the autumn of 1984 – a comment he now dismisses as flippant.

Twelve

The King and Us

Writing and recording was the order of spring 1987 for Neil and Chris. In May they received the 'Best International Hit' award for 'West End Girls' at the Ivor Novello awards. 15 June saw the release of 'It's a Sin', their first single of the year. On the flipside was 'You Know Where You Went Wrong'. The single was available in 7-inch and 12-inch formats, with the 12-inch version featuring a special extended disco mix of 'It's a Sin', coupled with the regular 7-inch B-sides. Both versions were produced by Julian Mendelsohn and mixed by Stephen Hague. A limited quantity of each format was made available in a special sleeve. The accompanying video for the single was shot in the London Docklands area and was directed by the eminent Derek Jarman, well known for his full-length films *Jubilee*, *The Tempest*, *Sebastiane* and *Caravaggio*. The single went on to top the UK chart and received similar success worldwide.

A special Ian Levine re-mix of the Number One hit was released on 6 July. The 12-inch version, available in a special sleeve, also featured 'You Know Where You Went Wrong' (rough mix), which the Boys produced in collaboration with Shep Pettibone. In addition, a cassette single of 'It's a Sin' became available. The limited edition cassette featured both 7-inch and original 12-inch versions of 'You Know Where You Went Wrong'. As this was released, the Boys were busy working on the next single, pencilled in for an August release date.

'Whilst Neil's voice continued to sound like Al Stewart, there's little doubt that "It's a Sin" will smash the charts wide open. It's the duo's most obvious European sounding song to date,' claimed the Blackpool *Evening Gazette*.

All this was proving a bit much for Neil, who said at the time, 'Frankly, it's rather embarrassing being a pop star or whatever. The people who hurl themselves into it, like Boy George, make the best stars. I would like to love publicity, to be able to give quotes every day of the week, to make things up about myself. But I'm not shameless enough. I'm not prepared to lie.'

Shortly after a plethora of good reviews, the Pet Shop Boys won a libel action against News Group Newspapers Limited and Jonathan King, who had indicated in the *Sun* that he felt 'It's a Sin' borrowed heavily from 'Wild World' by Cat Stevens. A Press release from the Parlophone offices stated the proceedings concerned articles which appeared in Mr King's 'Bizarre' columns published in the *Sun* newspaper in June and July 1987. 'In his columns Mr King alleged that Pet Shop Boys had infringed copyright of Cat Stevens' song "Wild World" by writing and recording their song "It's a Sin". The newspaper accepted this was untrue and have agreed to make an unqualified apology and retraction. News Group Newspapers and Mr King have agreed to pay substantial damages to a charity nominated by Pet Shop Boys, and to pay all Pet Shop Boys legal costs.'

A donation was made to the Jefferiss Research Wing Trust, an AIDS research unit and charity based at London's St Mary's Hospital.

Although he would not be drawn on the issue, globetrotting music personality Jonathan King told me, 'The Pet Shop Boys to me are always a bit of a problem because they veer towards being staggeringly good and clever in bursts and absolutely ghastly in other bursts. They are not of those bands that I consider on an ordinary level. They are very much up and down. Some of the things they do I think, "That's fabulous, what a clever idea and how well they've done it."

' "Always on my Mind" is a prime example and, funnily enough, is a song I was going to do a cover of years earlier. I was always aware of the need for a good new version. The Boys' version was absolutely perfect. It was exactly right for the time and the treatment. The first time I heard it I fell deeply in love with it.

'But then there will be other things they'll do and I think, "Oh my God, that doesn't work at all." And then there will be projects they will get into, like the Liza Minnelli album, which had that fabulous track on it that was a smash hit single, "Losing my Mind", and then all the rest which veered again towards being some very clever, nice ideas. "Rent" was very clever. "Twist in my Sobriety" I hated, although lots of other people loved it. So the Pet Shop Boys affect me in extremes. I very rarely think, "Oh yes, that's all right. It'll pass by." '

As the donation was made to the research foundation, the Boys were pleading poverty, according to the *Daily Mirror*, blaming their monetary predicament on lawsuits with record producer Bobby Orlando. Neil admitted to the paper: 'We have made a lot of money – but for other people.' According to the *Mirror*, despite the duo's worldwide achievements, with sales of three million singles and album chart success, Neil was still living in a one-bedroomed flat in South London. 'People tend to think we've both got £2 million mansions in Hampstead. But it's not like that,' he commented.

It was possibly in that same London flat that Neil received an early morning call bringing him the welcome news that 'It's a Sin' had gone to Number One after two weeks, dislodging the Firm. It was the Pet Shop Boys' second number one after 'West End Girls' in January 1986. 'It's fantastic, really great,' said Neil. 'I got a phone call at seven-forty a.m. – we weren't expecting to be Number One. We thought the "Star Trekking" record would still be there. It is great, as I didn't think we would make it.'

As if on cue, Neil's almost dour indifference shone through when he commented: 'Just because you're at Number One doesn't mean you have to be in a good mood.' He even admitted that things were not always rosy between the duo: 'Chris is a very moody person and he sulks a lot. When he's in a bad mood there's just no talking to him.

'Our biggest argument ever was one day we were doing some radio jingles. Chris didn't want to do it and kept speaking too fast and putting on silly voices. He was driving me mad! But when I got annoyed he thought I was being bossy, and in the end I just slammed down my headphones and stormed out.

'The only trouble was, I was trying to be dignified but our engineer had seen the whole row and thought it was the funniest thing he'd ever seen. So I swept out, there he was doubled up and screaming with laughter!'

Always one to be different, Neil chose his Catholic upbringing for the basis of the song. 'It is an unusual subject for a pop record, but we always try to have something fairly unusual. I think everyone is very, very influenced for all their life by their childhood and upbringing. I suppose it was a very powerful influence when I was brought up a Catholic. Once a Catholic always a Catholic – it's very true.'

Neil calls 'It's a Sin' ecclesiastical hi-NRG, with thunderclaps and whatever else involved. 'That doesn't mean we're making fun of Catholicism though, we're taking it all quite seriously.' The song is one of the Pet Shop Boys' oldest numbers, and was one of those originally worked on with Bobby Orlando in New York.

The Boys decided to tear apart the original and add extra sections, including an entire section recorded in Brompton Oratory in London.

'We went along there and turned the tape on even though there was no one there but a man cleaning the candlesticks,' remembers Neil. 'When we got back to the studio and played it we found we'd got this incredible booming ambience, even though we hadn't been taping anything in particular. That's running all the way through the record. Then there's "Amen", which is taken from when we went to Westminster Cathedral and taped these boys singing. We had to keep on making sure we felt like royals, but we did put some money in the Cathedral restoration fund box once.'

In fact Neil paid his first visit in two years to a Catholic church soon after the release of the single. 'A lot of people expect it to be far more exotic than it is. It had changed so much since I last went. They go expecting everything in Latin, incense and vestments, when what's far more likely is English services, Spanish guitar and some ghastly folk hymns. It's not the same as it was, and maybe the spirit of the song draws upon quite a romanticized Catholicism.'

For the accompanying video, Derek Jarman drew on a dazzling theatrical affair. 'What it is is that I had an idea for ages about being burnt at the stake in a video, like Joan of Arc or something, so we did this one which is set in the Middle Ages and in which I play an heretic. Chris plays the jailer and then there's this group of thirteen monks who are trying me and deciding whether I'm guilty,' says Neil. 'We used Ron Moody as the chief monk because he's got the sort of face that you imagine monks must have had then. Meanwhile, there's all these people representing each of the Seven Deadly Sins – Envy, Pride, Avarice, Lust, Greed, Anger and Sloth.

'Stephen Linard, the designer, plays Envy, and the painter, Duggie Fields, plays Avarice. There's all these strange characters wandering around reflecting what they're portraying. Greed even eats her costume.'

It was only during the filming of the video that Neil admitted that he realized what the Seven Deadly Sins were. He had not expected to find Anger and Pride in there. 'They're ones that I'm sure everybody indulges in. We certainly do,' he quipped.

'It's funny, but you still get worried about doing things that might be considered wrong or sacrilegious. Most Catholics that lapse do so because there's just so much to live up to in the religion. We always make the best rebels because there's so much to rebel against, but you can never quite stop that old residue of Catholicism remaining.'

Neil is featured in the video saying three 'Hail Mary's'. This from the pop star who, when he was growing up, wanted to be the Pope. 'I was very impressed by all the glamour attached to it, the costumes, but I was a devout Catholic. Then you find as an adolescent that everything you want to do is a sin,' he says.

'I thought I wanted to be Father Tennant and how good it would be to be eventually known as Saint Neil. When I was an altar boy I told my Mum of my plans. She said I should wait until I was sixteen.'

'It's a Sin', he said, was really about guilt. 'When I was growing up I thought everything that was any good was a sin. When people ask me, "Do I believe in God?" I always say "No". That's my stock answer. But, deep down, I think I'm lying.'

What Neil had not anticipated was the furore the song would create within the confines of the staffroom at St Cuthbert's Roman Catholic Grammar School. Such inspiration placed him well and truly in the doghouse with his former schoolmasters. The words were seen as a direct attack on the religious values preached by the teachers and priests at St Cuthbert's.

A spokesman for the school said the song was a gross misrepresentation of life at the school and the Catholic faith. A member of staff, who remembered teaching Tennant, said, 'It is very unfortunate that Neil has painted this distorted picture of his schooldays and the things he was taught. It is very hurtful. It is a long time since he was here and there have been a lot of changes since then in the Church. But even back in the Sixties when he came here we were quite open and forward-thinking. It certainly wasn't all hellfire and damnation.

'The message of Jesus is one of forgiveness. As Neil says in his song, Our Heavenly Father will forgive him. But it would perhaps have been better if he had considered the hurt his song would cause before he recorded it.'

During Neil's time at the all-boys school, the senior staff were all priests, who actively encouraged the pupils to attend

Mass several times a week, and placed heavy emphasis on religious teaching. Confession sessions were held every lunchtime. The line in the song: 'Father forgive me' is straight out of the Catholic confessional rite.

Former pupil Chris Baines, of Cochrane Park, Newcastle, said, 'There was a lot of religion in the school but I never realized he [Neil] was so bothered by it. The priests were all right. We used to have a lot of good laughs with them.'

Not this time, it would appear.

Neil's mother, Sheila, was naturally very quick to jump to her son's defence, as she commented to the Newcastle *Sunday Sun*, 'I think the school took the song out of context. I thought it was a lovely song. In fact it is my favourite Pet Shop Boys song.'

Neil revealed at this time that they were making plans for a possible tour in 1988 which would include his home town, once the finances had been properly sorted out, and told journalist Tim Pedley that for the previously planned tour, they had wanted to include two international opera singers 'for something a little bit different'.

'But when we costed it out we would lose a fortune and we don't want to do a conventional tour. If we can't do that we don't want to do anything else,' he said. The plan, apparently, was for something special, not just an ordinary rock show.

Ever ones to maintain their image, however low key, the Boys drew the line at a suggestion from trendy producer Janet Street-Porter that they should wear brown paper bags for her Saturday morning television show 'Get Fresh'. The idea was that the live studio audience would have to guess who the special celebrities were. An outraged Chris Lowe told the *Daily Mirror*: 'Producers can make you enter into totally undignified situations. We couldn't go through with it. It would have been far too embarrassing.'

One thing they were happy to go through with was an appearance on the UK television special 'Love Me Tender', which marked the tenth anniversary of the death of Elvis

Presley. The duo performed 'Always on my Mind' for the show on 14 August.

Later, visiting Paris for some special television promotional appearances, the Boys became casualties of a different kind. One show was running late and they had to cut across to the other side of the city for the next one. Neil told the *Sun*: 'We couldn't get a cab, but then someone rustled up an ambulance. They must have misunderstood, though, because we were taken to a casualty unit.'

For many, the sight of Neil on vocals and Chris behind the synthesizers on 'Top of the Pops' during the year brought memories flooding back of a similar duo with Blackpool connections: Soft Cell – with Blackpool's David Ball on synthesizer and Leeds' Marc Almond on vocals – had been there with 'Tainted Love'.

Soft Cell's music was also from bedsit-angstland: emotional traumas from two other taciturn, post-modernist stars. Chris went to the same school as David Ball, and puts the Pet Shop Boys in the same tradition as their latter-day charters, even down to them being a synth duo. He does not agree, however, that they sing about the same things. 'We've never been about sleaze. We're a bit seedy, perhaps, but never sleazy. And we write pop songs, while their pop songs have always been more incidental.'

The Boys have been placed in the same category as Soft Cell, New Order and the Human League for their contrary natures. Says Neil, 'We have the same attitude. We don't want to be part of the pop circus. There are some people who want to be professional pop stars, who want to be in the papers and to be screamed at. We decided not to go for that deliberately.

'I think it's part of being Northern. We're all similar. Soft Cell came from Blackpool and Leeds. New Order from Manchester, Human League from Sheffield, and we're from Blackpool and Newcastle. It's not just having a down-to-earth attitude, it's doing what you want. Otherwise you lose your dignity. You end up being made a fool of – I've seen that happen. We're more famous in America for turning things down than anything else.'

Soft Cell did it their way with phenomenal success. 'Tainted Love' set an all-time record of forty-five weeks in the US music charts, shattering Bill Haley's 1955 mark of forty-two weeks with 'Rock Around the Clock'. This from a duo who had titled their debut album *Non-Stop Erotic Cabaret*, and included compositions such as 'Sex Dwarf' and 'Seedy Films'. Thus, Chris's comment about sleaze.

Techno-pop synth wizard David Ball was stunned by Soft Cell's popularity, as he stated at the time of their success: 'When it comes to rock music, America tends to be much more conservative than Britain, very slow to take up new things. The US music scene seems so jaded and full of clichés. There are some fantastic artists doing interesting things in America but they don't happen commercially.'

Like the Pet Shop Boys, Soft Cell was almost embarrassed by its success, claiming: 'We basically reject the pomp, the pretension and the pose of rock 'n' roll. The whole music business has changed completely since the Sixties – there's so much more music going on and so many more bands. Instead of ten massive acts, you have fifty that enjoy much more moderate success. Yet people keep looking for the new Beatles, the new Rolling Stones, the new David Bowie. That kind of success just doesn't exist any more.'

Soft Cell described their dance music as 'mutated minimal electronic disco'. Almond personally called it a 'dirty garage sound'. According to Ball, they set out to write honest songs that dealt with mundane, everyday things. 'Too many pop bands write stuff that doesn't mean anything, made-up fairy tales that bear no relation to people's lives. People find some of our songs embarrassing simply because they're so honest, because they see themselves in the lyrics in a way they don't like. That's not to say our songs are unromantic. Pop is about romance, but there's a lot of romance about your first grotty apartment. It's something young people everywhere understand.'

The young related to Soft Cell like they relate to the Pet Shop Boys today. There are definite parallels, not only in their musical inventiveness, but also in their jealously guarded privacy. Like the Pet Shop Boys, Ball and Almond kept themselves and their lives under wraps.

Unlike Neil and Chris, Soft Cell were not averse to the occasional random show. The adrenalin flowed on stage — stimulating for the duo and exciting for the audience. Atmosphere and feelings were more important than perfection. They got a kick from playing in a sleazy atmosphere. The Pet Shop Boys are as far removed from that as they can possibly be.

As *Record Collector* noted, 'At a time when it is said there is a solid move away from drum machines and synthesizers back to guitars and proper drum kits, the Pet Shop Boys have proved that to sell records, it doesn't necessarily take profound lyrics, musical complexity or a desire to swim with the tide. In sticking to an economical formula of a simple beat overlaid with a catchy lyric, Tennant has proved his own point that "pop music is rubbish in a good way", for the Pet Shop Boys have stripped it down to its bare minimum and, in terms of chart successes, have shown that simplest can often be best.'

Commenting on the possibility of a tour, *Record Collector* stated, 'It will be interesting to see how well the duo can keep up the nonchalant, aloof image portrayed so well in their videos. Like Soft Cell and Bronski Beat before them, fans will be wondering how their music will develop in a way that will please both old fans and attract new converts, for the small synth-based units tend not to enjoy lengthy lifespans. The Pet Shop Boys' down-to-earth approach to pop music, and grasp of what the record-buying public really wants, indicate that they will be around for a good while yet.'

Thirteen

The Springfield Connection

In the build-up to Christmas 1984, Neil and Chris sat down and wrote the song 'What Have I Done to Deserve This?' with songwriter Allee Williams, an established wordsmith who had penned Earth, Wind and Fire's 'Boogie Wonderland'. The following year found the Boys recording their debut album with Stephen Hague. They wanted to include 'What Have I Done to Deserve This?' but they needed someone to sing the other half of the duet. Suggested names came out of the hat, but none had exactly what the Boys were looking for.

'We wanted a woman with a voice suggesting both experience and vulnerability, warmth but also a tough take-it-or-leave-it attitude,' said Neil to the *Evening Standard*. 'The song is neither teenage romance nor nostalgia, but a dialogue about the end of an affair between two adults. Nikki, our manager's assistant, had a bright idea. "What about Dusty Springfield? I thought she was your favourite singer . . ." '

Neil had, in fact, mentioned on several occasions that his favourite album was the 1968 *Dusty in Memphis*, feeling that it captured her heart-breaking voice within a soul context and established her as the only authentic white female soul singer of the era. Before her album Dusty had received worldwide recognition for hits such as 'I Only Want To Be With You', 'I Just Don't Know What To Do With Myself', 'You Don't Have To Say You Love Me', and 'I Close My Eyes and Count To Ten'.

'Her breathy, glamorous voice was always thrilling, even when the Sixties pop industry tried to cram her into a conventional showbusiness, cabaret career, alongside Cilla Black, Lulu and Anita Harris. And, like every great pop singer, she had more than a great voice; she had a look – the blonde bouffant hair-do, the black eye make-up . . . acres of it,' eulogized Neil.

Following the success of the single 'Son of a Preacher Man' from the album *Dusty in Memphis*, her career took a downward turn, despite several album releases in the Seventies. She moved to America, and most of the world forgot about her. She later signed to Peter Stringfellow's Hippodrome label with no success. By 1985 she had become a somewhat lost legend. Neil had heard the rumours that Dusty was living the life of a recluse, with only her cats and her memories for company, and never thought she would agree to work with them. So, with fingers crossed, a tape of the song was sent to her manager in America. 'We weren't sure what reaction we would get. After all, we didn't even know if she had heard of us,' said Neil. The answer, several weeks later, was a great disappointment. Dusty was not interested. As a result, the song never made it on to the Boys' debut album.

'Then, several months later, her manager phoned our manager. She wants to do it. Do they still want her to do it? Yes, we did. When?' recalls Neil. The Boys, naturally, were knocked out. Just before Christmas 1986, Dusty boarded a plane in Los Angeles and joined the Boys in a London recording studio. Dressed in black leather designer jacket and high-heeled boots, with blonde hair and black eye make-up, she arrived carrying the lyric sheet of the song, annotated and underlined. The Boys were nothing if not impressed.

'Chris, Stephen and I began to consult with the legend about how to sing our song and she was very nice, surprisingly a little lacking in self-confidence. As if by telepathy, a Dusty fan appeared on the studio doorstep and was invited in to listen. Dusty's English secretary arrived bearing a new compilation cassette. "They keep repackaging the old songs," the legend marvelled. Then she went through to sing,' said Neil.

'Her voice was the same as ever. When she sang her solo part everyone in the control room smiled. She sounded just like she used to. Breathy, warm, thrilling. Like Dusty Springfield. "Is that the sort of thing you want?" she asked.

'Later we chatted in the studio about how she loves all the recording technology – if only they'd had all that years ago when she couldn't get the sounds she wanted; about how she'd had laryngitis throughout the recording of *Dusty in Memphis*, and that's why she sounded the way she did. She chuckled, then said she was jet-lagged and went back to her hotel.'

Dusty later told the magazine *City Limits*, 'They were so different. Thank God I'm so versatile. They didn't want me to do anything, they just wanted the sound of my voice. It was that simple!'

When the Boys first announced to their record company that they wanted Dusty to sing on the track, a voice complained, 'No one's interested in her any more.'

How wrong people can be.

'The producer couldn't understand why we wanted Dusty when he could persuade Tina Turner to sing on the album,' said Neil. 'But Dusty is one of my favourite singers. Her voice is still tremendous, but when the record company heard that we were doing the song with Dusty, they freaked out. A good sign – we're always worried when the record company likes something.'

At the age of forty-eight, Dusty proved to the world that she still had it in her, as the single, which was released on 10 August, soared to Number Two in the charts. It was available in 7-inch, 12-inch and cassette single formats, and all were produced by Stephen Hague. The 12-inch and cassette singles featured two special re-mixes of 'What Have I Done To Deserve This?' – an extended mix by Julian Mendelsohn and a disco mix by Shep Pettibone. The B-side was produced by the Pet Shop Boys and David Jacob.

Of her fans, she told *City Limits*, 'They just won't let me go. That was twenty years ago – but the fans don't want you to change, and some get quite resentful if you do. My Sixties image is part of their growing up. But I'm different now, I don't want to be exactly what I was.'

Clearly, she was as popular as ever, and Phonogram took the bait. On 12 January 1988, the record company released *Dusty Springfield – The Silver Collection*, a celebration of her twenty-fifth year as a successful solo artist. It coincided with the release of her single, the re-issued 'I Only Want To Be With You', her first-ever hit, which was being used in the national television advertising campaign for Britvic-55 orange juice. The compilation featured all her eighteen solo hits, ten of which had made it to the Top Ten.

A little over a year later, on 13 February 1989, Parlophone released the single 'Nothing Has Been Proved', especially written for Dusty by the Pet Shop Boys, who co-produced and guested on the track, which was the theme from the Palace Pictures film, *Scandal*, based on the John Profumo affair, and starring Ian McKellen, Joanne Whalley-Kilmer and Bridget Fonda. Composer Carl Davis created the film's score. The Boys had, in fact, written two songs for Dusty for the film. 'In Private' had been rejected by the film-makers because they thought it sounded too contemporary.

In addition to the 7-inch single, a 12-inch dance re-mix by Marshall Jefferson was available, together with an instrumental version. The orchestral arrangement on the track was by Angelo Badalamenti, who composed and conducted the music for *Blue Velvet* and who arranged the orchestration on the Boys' forthcoming album *Actually*. All the versions were co-produced by Julian Mendelsohn.

Neil told the *Star* on 7 August, 'We think the single is going to be a big, big, hit. We have both admired her voice for a long time and were thrilled when she agreed to come and work with us. We felt honoured. It was a great experience.'

The Boys' collaboration with Dusty on her most recent album, *Reputation*, received mixed reviews. *Melody Maker*'s Paul Lester commented, 'The trouble with this album is we know too much about Dusty Springfield to be convinced by the impassioned outpourings that the Pet Shop Boys obviously think she brings to their music. Less famous people often act more effectively as a blank emotional canvas for the listener to identify with . . . The whole of side two was produced by Tennant and Lowe and, with the exception of the ugly strutting electro-stomp of "In Private", the chaps acquit themselves well. But, as far as PSB ventures go, the "I'm Not Scared" team-up with Patsy Kensit remains easily the best.'

Andrew Collins, writing in the *New Musical Express*, said the Tennant-Lowe contribution on side two was the more satisfying. 'On supreme PSB stuff like "Daydreaming" (for which Dusty impersonates Tennant's spoken-verse style to magnificent, sultry effect) and "Nothing Has Been Proved" (that *Scandal* theme with the, well, cinematic hi-drama feel) Dusty's seasoned brilliance is allowed to luxuriate in that now-familiar electro-upholstery.'

As Dusty flew into London from Los Angeles to film the accompanying video for 'What Have I Done To Deserve This?', the Boys were wrapping up their next album, which was due for release the following month.

The Pets became upset over a sex scene which had been filmed for the video. The problem was over a sequence which starred a real-life courting couple. Lovers Rod O'Grady and model Jane Spencer were seen in each other's arms on a large motorbike. The Boys wanted the scene axed.

A set insider said: 'They [Neil and Chris] also believe the bike scene has worked out far too raunchy, and is not in keeping with their sophisticated, sensitive image.'

Fourteen

Actually . . . It's Brilliant

The Seventh of September saw the release of the long-awaited album, *Actually*, which was recorded in London at Sarm West and Advision studios. It contained ten tracks, including the recent Number One, 'It's a Sin' and the current single 'What Have I Done To Deserve This?', at the time lying at Number Five in the charts. The Boys collaborated on three of the tracks. 'One More Chance' was written with Bobby Orlando, 'What Have I Done to Deserve This?' with Allee Williams, and 'It Couldn't Happen Here' with Ennio Morricone, one of the world's most renowned soundtrack composers. The latter track also featured an orchestral arrangement by Angelo Badalementi. All the remaining tracks were penned by Neil and Chris. Julian Mendelsohn was responsible for the production of five tracks, and other producers included Stephen Hague, David Jacob, Shep Pettibone and Andy Richards.

As it transpired, the word 'actually' was simply one they use a great deal. According to Chris at the time, 'We were thinking of calling it "Jollysight" actually, which was the name of a hotel we saw in Italy – so that, when people asked why, we could say, "because it's a jolly sight better than the last one." '

I wrote in the *Daily Express* at the time, 'Pops overlords strut over a parade ground of regimented perfection. Purposeful and direct, it is a lifeline to post modernity. "Hit Music" (one of the tracks) is deliberately shaped around the "Peter Gunn" riff – glossy, naughty, but nice. The album delicately embraces imagination and conceptual charm. Actually . . . it's brilliant.'

It was if the duo were operating from a hit factory, although they were quick to admit that not everything they touched had turned to gold. 'Love Comes Quickly' had peaked at Number 19, while 'Opportunities' reached Number 11. As Neil observed: 'Everything Madonna does turns to gold. But I get quite annoyed when we're called one-hit wonders, although I think it was quite a reasonable assumption to make in the beginning – because whenever I hear something new, I think the same.

'What people don't seem to realize is a lot of our earnings disappear before we see them.'

Ten days earlier, the Boys were in America on a promotional tour, where 'It's a Sin' – which reached Number One in seven European countries – was in the Top Forty. They were due to move up country to Canada for radio and television appearances and were highly amused when reports filtered through that they were about to split, as reported in the *Sun* on 17 September. 'PET SHOP BOYS IN VIDEO STORM' screamed the headline, as Kevin O'Sullivan exclusively reported: 'Top rock duo the Pet Shop Boys had a massive bust-up over their latest pop video, it was revealed last night.

'Now the future of the Boys is in doubt,' wrote O'Sullivan, 'despite their amazing success with two Number One hits and their current Number Eight smash "What Have I Done To Deserve This?" '

Allegedly, Chris Lowe was too tired to attend the shoot, and the *Star* also reported the same sequence of events. The video was, however, eventually completed so these allegations may be unfounded.

A source apparently close to the band told the *Star*, 'There was a big bust-up because Chris didn't turn up for the video. He was very tired . . . but a lot of money was at stake.'

'Rent', with the flipside 'I Want a Dog', was released on 12 October. It made Number Eight and the Boys spent a fortnight promoting it in Japan. The single was re-mixed from the Boys platinum album *Actually* by Stephen Hague, and was available in three formats – 7-inch, 12-inch and cassette single. The latter two formats featured extended and dub versions of 'Rent', re-mixed by François Kevorkian, plus 'I Want a Dog', produced by the Pet Shop Boys. All the versions of 'Rent' were produced by Julian Mendelsohn.

On 11 October the Boys performed 'Rent' on London Weekend Television's fully networked 'Live from the Palladium' show after returning from Canada where 'It's a Sin' was riding in the Top Thirty singles chart. The Boys were also mid-way through working on the film set of 'It Couldn't Happen Here' directed by Jack Bond, and starring the bubbly actress Barbara Windsor.

The Boys had just turned down an offer to work on the soundtrack to a new Stephen Spielberg film called *Inner Space* after they discovered that other stars like Rod Stewart and Wang Chung had also been approached. 'We didn't want to be on a compilation with loads of other groups,' said the Boys to *News On Sunday*.

Barbara Windsor was far from impressed with their Palladium performance, as she says: 'When I saw them I told Chris off. I said, "If you are going to do the Palladium, you have got to do it properly." The performance was OK but when the curtain came down, Neil bowed and Chris just walked off. It was all half-hearted and I said they couldn't do that – not at the Palladium. "You are not in some club or playing at a concert where you can do what you like," I told them.'

At this juncture they had never toured, rarely agreed to interviews and, according to Sheryl Garrett in *News on Sunday*, they have even admitted to having a reputation for being 'awkward, miserable bastards'. But, even so, by being awkward they had kept a firm grip on their sanity and their careers. 'If it has our name on it, we like to make sure it's of a certain quality,' said Chris Lowe.

Even so, pop's seemingly most miserable duo could hardly

raise a smile for the Palladium, and poor compère Jimmy Tarbuck was left almost speechless after the performance. They even carried their glum approach on to the album cover of *Actually*, which shows Neil Tennant yawning. But, says Neil, 'I thought the cover of *Actually* was very funny but some people have taken it really personally.

'*New Musical Express* said, "How could you trust someone who yawns on their cover?" But they never ask how you could trust someone who makes themselves look as pretty as possible, which is what most groups working in pop music do.'

By November 'It's a Sin' had climbed to Number Nine in the States and the album *Actually* had made the US Number 25 slot. On 30 November, in time for the Christmas record-buying spree, the Pet Shop Boys' first-ever cover version hit the shops with the release of 'Always on my Mind', originally released by Elvis Presley in 1972 and which reached Number Nine in the singles chart in December of that year. It was the song the Boys had chosen to record as their contribution to Central Television's Presley tribute the previous 15 August. Of the many performers on the show, the Boys were the only ones to produce their own track and their re-working of the Presley classic became, for many, the highlight of the show. The success of this project prompted Neil and Chris to re-record the track with producer Julian Mendelsohn, who also re-mixed the song for the 12-inch extended dance mix. The Boys wrote and produced a new song for the B-side, entitled 'Do I Have To?'

Christmas is a time for family togetherness, and someone very much on Neil's mind at this time was his father Bill, who had entered hospital for a hip operation, but who was allowed home for the festive holiday. So it was that Neil joined Bill, his mother Sheila, brother Philip and sister Susan around the table for turkey and crackers before settling down to watch himself on 'Top of the Pops', just prior to the Queen's speech to the nation. Yes, the Number One son had returned to Gosforth.

Mum Sheila exclaimed to the *Sunday Sun*, 'It is tremendously exciting having Neil at Number One at Christmas. It is the time of the year when all the top singers and groups want to be on "Top of the Pops". I was on tenterhooks listening to the charts, hoping he would make it.

'Fame has not changed Neil at all. He is a quiet boy, although he does get the opportunity to do a lot more travelling now.'

The Pet Shop Boys had fought off a strong challenge in the BBC/Gallup chart from Rick Astley's re-make of the Nat King Cole classic, 'When I Fall in Love', but he lost sales ground when the original was re-released for Christmas. Astley slipped down two places to four, and despite a tremendous surge upwards of thirteen places, the Nat King Cole original had to settle for the Number Seven spot.

The Boys' year was capped when they knocked everyone else for six by being voted Best Group of the Year in the *Sun*'s 'Bizarre' readers' poll. 'They have proved all it takes is good, classy music to make it big. And they certainly had that with chart-busters like "It's a Sin", "What Have I Done To Deserve This?" and "Always on my Mind",' declared the paper on 29 December. The Boys also got the sixth-best single and the fourth-best album nominations.

'Congratulations, lads! Now, when are you two going to play live?' queried the *Sun*. As it happened, an awful lot of other people were beginning to ask that very same question.

Fifteen

It Couldn't Happen Here

Pop stars, it has to be said, have built themselves an extremely bad reputation in the world of film. So what made the Pet Shop Boys presume that they could fare any better than their contemporaries is anyone's guess. But they were prepared to give it a go. Why not? The promotional videos for their singles had proved extremely popular. Euro pop on vinyl with its irresistible dance groove was one thing. Pop's woodentops on video to pop's woodentops on film. And eighty-seven minutes long? That was another. Their apparent unwillingness to tour obviously played a hand in the decision. If they weren't prepared to play the white man's game, then they would do it another way. So they looked into the possibility of a stage show, with sets, dancers, actors, the works, and concluded that they would have to dig far too deeply into their pockets to make it work.

Neil admitted that anything else would probably be boring. What was the appeal of watching an entirely electronic, recording-studio-based group with only a keyboard player and a singer pretend to play their records at a venue such as Wembley Arena?

So it was that the head of production at Picture Music International – the visual arm of EMI Music – Chips Chipperfield, came up with the suggestion of a narrative film. Jack Bond's name was also mentioned as director. Bond had been involved in profiles of Roald Dahl and Patricia Highsmith for television's 'The South Bank Show', blending a documentary style with fictional narrative, which

Chipperfield thought would translate well into a pop music format.

'We met Jack for dinner on several occasions and we went to really expensive restaurants on the budget,' said Chris to the *Sunday Times*. According to Neil, 'The first thing he said was, "Do you like taking risks?" and we said, "No!" He said, "Do you like to live your life on the edge?" We said, "No!" He said, "Good!" '

Originally conceived as an hour-long video based around the album *Actually*, it was decided that they would draw on their worldwide hits such as 'West End Girls', 'Always on my Mind', 'What Have I Done To Deserve This?' and 'It's a Sin' for the soundtrack. The film was entitled 'It Couldn't Happen Here', and, as the Press material informed us, took the form of a musical allegory, where the comic and the dangerous go hand in hand . The storyline takes the form of a journey across England, passing through the incredible, the ordinary and the visually bizarre – well suited to the talents of the highly acclaimed Jack Bond. It was set at the seaside because that setting had been important in both their childhoods.

Bond had first joined BBC-TV as a creator of promotional trailers, with the freedom to write and direct sequences to represent both drama and documentaries. He was then invited to direct films for the BBC, before entering the world of theatre with his surrealistic musical production of Jane Arden's *The Gas Oven* starring Victor Spinetti and Sheila Allen. Steadily, he built a sound reputation for his creative writing skills and entrepreneurial, technical imagery.

His dazzling style and often over-indulgence was seemingly perfect for the Boys' modern-day version of the Beatles film, *Hard Days Night*.

'It Couldn't Happen Here' begins with childhood memories in a windswept, decaying seaside resort. Neil and Chris take leave of a smothering landlady (played by Barbara Windsor, famed for her *Carry On* films) who leads morning prayers over mountainous breakfasts, a novelty salesman (played by Gareth Hunt of 'The Avengers' fame) with a crude line in humour, and an ominous blind priest (Joss Ackland) warning of hellfire and damnation, as his young pupils escape to sample the erotic delights of dancing nuns in the resort's seedy pier theatre. During the film, characters pop out of cupboards to harass, threaten and amuse.

According to Jack Bond, 'To me this film tells a story in that it's a journey across England; if you like, it's an impressionistic journey of memories; to some extent, the memories that I have of England, and all our memories, are formed in childhood. In the film there was a coming together of the way I saw people and situations in this country and the way the Pet Shop Boys did, and we talked about it before starting the film.'

In the film, a quilt-making mother uses her loneliness as a weapon. A simple car drive turns into a supposed nightmare when a murderous hitch-hiker (Joss Ackland) is picked up, looking suspiciously like their childhood mentor, a blind priest. Ackland looks manic enough, but Chris Lowe plays his part as the front-seat passenger so superbly laidback that he almost falls out of the old two-tone Ford Consul.

Another scene featured on the video is that of a man on fire, captured leaving his home for a normal day at the office, briefcase in hand. The scene is a backdrop to the song 'King's Cross', taken from the album *Actually*. The scene was obviously shot a long time before the horrific King's Cross fire in London, which claimed over thirty lives, but it became a chilling prophecy.

A meal in a transport café is interrupted by a jaded thespian ventriloquist, superbly played by Gareth Hunt, and his manic dummy, which he takes out of his battered blue suitcase and seats opposite him. The dummy starts talking to Chris, who is happily swilling back a plateful of oysters – in a transport café!

At the end of a train journey, Neil and Chris are met by a poisonous courtier, who chauffeurs them to their final destination, a night club in the wastelands of a fire-filled war zone, where zombie-like creatures dance the night away as Neil pleads into the night air, '... Just give me one more chance.'

Jack Bond, co-writer James Dillon, Neil and Chris got their heads together round the table for enthusiastic bursts of script-writing, at which time they would thrash out ideas and talk through common experiences. The only acting role in which Neil refused to participate was going up on a circular wheel at night; at the time of filming, it was being battered by a heavy wind and was quite unsafe. Compliments Jack Bond, 'I would say they are the easiest people I've worked with in my whole life. They were just intensely hard-working professionals out to do a good job.'

Whether or not pop music lends itself to the medium of an eighty-seven-minute-long film was something Jack Bond had to discover for himself. He admits that when he first embarked on the project he was undecided, but it wasn't long before he was converted to the fact that it could, in this case, work. 'With this film the music became the theme music for the scenes. It wasn't a lavish adherence to, "How do we visualize a series of songs?" It was very much a film and the music carried the film. More and more I see the strength of it. The film doesn't have a strong narrative line – it's somewhat surrealist and somewhat broken up in structure. And yet it does make sense. But I think the English have always resisted surrealist work, if this is a surrealist work.'

Bond thought the film would be dubbed surreal, although to him it is a totally ordinary story told in visual shorthand through the strength of the music – 'It enabled me to drop what I saw as mundane dialogue scenes to tell the story, and to work in a visual shorthand and use extraordinary-looking shots to convey what would have otherwise taken me a more pedestrian form of writing to achieve. I think the music gave me that freedom.'

Although there are various references to evil in the film, according to Jack Bond the Lucifer references are only significant in terms of a hellfire figure – someone who instills fear in children through heavy religious upbringing – yet it has no malign or obscure intentions. 'It's a Catholic version of hellfire preaching to make young children feel a sense of guilt at an early age. But there is no evil present in the film – not in my eyes, anyway,'

Bond saw the film as a kind of warning: that if we sail along serenely, just making adaptations to the world around us, then it becomes dangerous. 'The promise that keeps us quiet is reward – reward being better homes, cars, more money, and success,' he says. 'The film is finally a warning against complacency; it ploughs inexorably towards violence at the end and following violence is a kind of mechanized state which is what the dancers have. They are functioning but that is all. They are clean, well-dressed; they seem to be confident – they even have smiles – but they are dead. I see Pet Shop Boys as a fairly aware symbol walking through all this.

'It's an allegory of past, present and future. It's rooted in the childhood past, I would say, of Pet Shop Boys and myself. It brings us up to the present day and takes a look at where we're going.'

Says Neil: 'It's very English. If it's in a tradition of pop music films it belongs with *Magical Mystery Tour* or the Dave Clark Five in *Catch Us if You Can*. It's not in the same tradition as *Summer Holiday* or *A Hard Day's Night* or *Purple Rain* or *Breaking Glass*.'

Chris complements that by saying: 'The film is very British. It reminds me of the whole Sixties attitude – those films in which everything's an icon. It couldn't possibly be an American film.'

Bond's impression of the Boys, having met them and listened to their material was that their music was all about memories. 'It's an episodic film. It has a story. It's not just an expression of music. It's also not fast cut in any way that is reminiscent of promos. It is cut in a feature film way, with no hurriedness. If you tried to run an hour or more with promo cutting, you'd drive yourself mad,' he told the *Sunday Times*.

The pressures of film work, the times of boredom, the scene-setting, were all taken in the Boys' stride. It took them away from their everyday pressures of promotional work – the constant ringing of the telephone. And it grew to be something more than they had at first anticipated – from a video of concert footage to a feature film.

Bond was impressed by their dedication: 'They're so unstarry. They enjoyed the commitment of going to work every day. They enjoyed that discipline. I imagine in music you can usually suit yourself more.'

One actress who has found herself in many a foolish situation on film is Barbara Windsor, whom Jack Bond wanted to play the parts of landlady and French maid in *It Couldn't Happen Here*. Barbara was no novice when it came to the bizarre, having worked with the eccentric director Ken Russell in the film *The Boyfriend*, in which she played Hortense.

Barbara first heard of the Pet Shop Boys' project when she received a telephone call from Gerald Thomas, the director of the *Carry On* movies. Bond had approached him at Pinewood Studios, saying that he was mad about Barbara and wanted to meet her. 'He said Jack Bond was doing this film with the Pretty Things,' recalls Barbara. 'Now I do know about pop music. I love it. I said it couldn't be them because they hadn't been around for years and they were never the biggest hit out of all those groups. Gerald described Jack Bond as being a bit like Ken Russell. Bond eventually contacted me and said he was doing a film with the Pet Shop Boys. I went to meet him and he wanted me to play this over-the-top landlady.'

Unfortunately, when Barbara saw the script, she could not make head or tail of much of it. 'It was like being with Ken Russell all over again,' she noted.

After she agreed to play the part of the landlady, Bond phoned Barbara and said he had come up with the idea of her playing a French maid as well. As Barbara agreed, more ideas for different roles came flooding in. So did the surprises. Bond told Barbara that all the filming would be carried out on location. 'I said it was wonderful because I never got to have any decent locations on the *Carry On* films,' she recalls. 'It was always the back lot at Pinewood or one night in Wales. It was awful. Then it transpired my locations for this film were a night shoot in Clacton and a day in Brixton.'

Neil and Chris arrived for the night shoot. Barbara had not met them before, although she knew their work. Everyone knew Barbara's work, too. 'It's the story of my life. I suppose because I have been going for so many years, and because I have worked with actresses like Joan Littlewood, people just say, "Get up and do it". I very rarely get directed or choreographed. After meeting Neil and Chris, Jack [Bond] wanted me to get up and just waft around them. There was no choreographer for me, although Wanda Rokicki [assistant to the film's choreographer, Arlene Phillips] was around. It wasn't as if I was working with dancers. It was a bit like doing a Ken Russell movie in that Jack fantasized about it.

'Neil and Chris were so sweet, and are great fans of the *Carry On*s. They were so thrilled that I had said yes to the film. They made me feel so good and thought it wonderful that I was in this caravan, getting changed and doing my make-up under dreadful conditions. It didn't matter. I said that all my life I had worked like that. Everyone says it's a glamorous life, but it isn't.'

The night shoot in Clacton in November 1987 was scheduled for ten o'clock. Barbara had risen at four a.m. and travelled down to the seaside resort. That same night she had to dress up as a French maid and, in the scene, kiss an extremely nervous Chris Lowe. 'It would have been fine for Chris if I had been twenty years younger, the poor darling, but there I was at fifty! But Chris was lovely.'

The next port of call was Brixton, where the cast prepared for an early morning shoot in a derelict house. This time Barbara had to dress as a landlady and serve Chris Lowe with a mountainous breakfast which, according to the script, she would end up wearing. As far as Barbara was concerned, it was worse than doing any *Carry On* movie. The food was cooked at nine a.m. and Barbara was eventually covered in it eight hours later. The mega-sized breakfast consisted of four large tins of baked beans, twenty eggs, twenty sausages, and tin upon tin of tomatoes. Unfortunately, when it came to the crunch, Chris could not go through with it. 'Chris said, "I can't do it to her; she's too lovely," ' recalls Barbara. 'Jack Bond turned round and said, "She's used to it. She made all those *Carry On* movies." As it so happens, I never got it in the chops. Joan Sims did, but not me.'

There was the added condition of getting the scene right first time, so Barbara tried to encourage Chris to go ahead, but to no avail. The crew had also forgotten that there were no facilities for Barbara to bathe after the shoot. 'I told them to continue and not to worry about it. I told them I would much prefer that to happen to me than play an attractive lady. I hate playing saucy blondes. That is hard work, believe it or not. Anyway, I said I was the one who would get the laugh,' recalls Barbara. No amount of persuasion would convince Chris to do it, though. So, in the end, he had to fake the scene, and it fell to Jack Bond to cover a game Barbara in food.

Barbara had only just begun wearing contact lenses, and having cleaned her eyes of various sauces, she had to be made up as Dusty Springfield. Earlier in her career Barbara had appeared on the Jack Jackson Show, where she would mime to Dusty records. Jack Jackson was not terribly impressed, as she recalls, 'He always used to say, "You're useless. You don't do it right." ' Be that as it may, Barbara got the mascara on and took her place on set at eleven o'clock at another house in Brixton. By this time her tired, sore eyes were streaming. 'It was really painful but it looked all right.' In fact, it looked particularly odd, with the mascara, curlers and hair net, and Barbara walking around the lounge, cordless telephone in hand, putting everything behind her duet with Chris on 'What Have I Done to Deserve This?'. She might well have wondered.

Between the Clacton and Brixton shoots, Neil and Chris were billed for the London Palladium when Chris fell foul of Barbara's tongue. Even so, the Boys had nothing but praise for Barbara and her co-stars Gareth Hunt and Joss Ackland for the way in which they were coaxed and led through their roles.

Despite the grim locations and the spectacular breakfast scene, Barbara enjoyed making the film with the Boys, and Jack Bond. Whereas she was used to doing one take, or two at the most on the *Carry On* set, Jack would expect her to repeat the scenes, over and over, but never specifically telling her what he wanted, until he felt it was right. 'He would suddenly say, out of the blue, "That's a take" and I would think *Why*? But Jack got the best out of me. The *Carry On* movies only played a minor part in my life, and it was lovely to be asked to do something different. It was also nice to be able to change the script. Everyone thinks that when we did the *Carry On*s it looked like we just went in on the day and got out there and did it. But, in fact, we would keep right to the script. Not one word was changed. With this film, you felt you had contributed. Gareth [Hunt] and I threw things in and took things out, which is good. I would certainly like to do something like this again. It was so different in one respect, yet it ended up being the same as I have always done, with regard to the freezing locations, the good laughs, and doing my own thing. At the end of the day, all I was was a landlady version of Barbara Windsor. I could play someone my age, and I don't often get a chance to do that.'

As for working with Neil and Chris, Barbara says, 'They are just nice, ordinary guys and I now watch their careers with great interest. I don't know why people always expect pop singers to be "way-out". The Boys didn't seem to come with the trappings of pop stars. Chris, particularly, is very shy, which is probably why he hides behind hats and dark glasses.' Barbara is, without a doubt, the only person ever to get away with calling them 'darlings'.

Throughout the month of April, the Boys were in Miami, where they had been recording with producer Lewis Martinee, of the Latin pop sound. The film was about to open in the States, and Neil commented, 'I'm a nervous wreck about the film. It's quite embarrassing being on the cinema screen.'

The Boys and the rest of the cast could not hide from the

reviews. The film received plenty of publicity, but not much of it encouraging. It may well have been better received if it had done the rounds of the art houses rather than the selected cinemas throughout Britain when it opened on 8 July 1988. At the time of its release, Jack Bond commented, 'It's unpredictable, totally unpredictable. And the last thing you're thinking of when you're making a film is how it will be received. It takes over and what you want to do takes over, and all you can do is hope people like it.'

Not everyone did. Under the crosshead 'DREADFUL', Alan Frank wrote in the *Star*, 'Fans of the Pet Shop Boys will doubtless enjoy *It Couldn't Happen Here*. But everyone else is advised to steer well clear of this dim and dismal film which simply resembles a series of dreadful pop videos.'

Ouch! The *Sunday Express* was of the same opinion, '*It Couldn't Happen Here* is a 22-carat stinker that resembles an over-extended pop video. A showcase for the popular Pet Shop Boys, it is a pretentious odyssey by the duo across England. Childhood memories feature prominently in the deliberately confusing scenario; so do several larger-than-life characters from their past. Don't ask me why It Couldn't Happen Here. It can. It did.'

The *Daily Express* stated, '*It Couldn't Happen Here* unfortunately did. Here it is, a pretentious fantasy spun around the pop group Pet Shop Boys' Neil Tennant and Chris Lowe. Directed by Jack Bond with all the bizarre foolishness of an immature Ken Russell, it consists of a series of situations in which the lads find themselves.'

Even Chris Lowe's local paper, the *Evening Gazette* slated their local hero's efforts: 'Not since the Beatles made *Magical Mystery Tour* has a rock film been more anxiously awaited than Pet Shop Boys' *It Couldn't Happen Here*. Unfortunately, not since that psychedelic-soaked multi-colour extravaganza has a rock film proved to be so ultimately disappointing (with the possible exception of Pink Floyd's *The Wall*).

'Blackpool's Chris Lowe and former journalist Neil Tennant have cornered the market in bedsit angst for the 1980s

Euro-pop generation – driving beats taking a succession of lyrically deliberately guilt-ridden songs to the top of the charts. All irresistible dance material and all well and good whilst kept on vinyl, tape or CD. Even when transferred to small-screen videos of but a few minutes duration the duo could do no wrong – but eighty-seven minutes?

'Arlene Phillips continues to walk her choreography on the thin line towards pornography with a raunchy interpretation of "It's a Sin" featuring the sort of dancing nuns of which Ken Russell would be proud and a less visually obvious version of "Rent". 'If ever a film had been consciously made to become a cult attraction then this is it . . . The last words as the closing credits roll are "Wake up, wake up." You may well have to.'

Even before the film was released, Joss Ackland had told the *Sun*, 'I only agreed to be in the video because one of my daughters is a big fan of theirs. I had no idea what was going on during filming. Let's face it, the whole thing was a load of cobblers.'

That wasn't the end of it. The *Star* wrote later, 'The Pet Shop Boys' debut movie, *It Couldn't Happen Here*, which bombed after only a week's run, has left everyone concerned severely skint.'

One thing the Boys had never had to do was hide from the public, who rarely recognized them. They continued to use the London Underground and walk the streets without being hassled. Even the security staff at the EMI offices in London's Manchester Square had tried on one occasion to stop Chris from entering, having mistaken him for a delivery man. And, during the filming of the scene for 'King's Cross', in *It Couldn't Happen Here*, members of the public were strategically placed with their Pet Shop Boys albums. Chris and Neil walked past. Neil heard one of them say, 'Is that them?' and the others said it wasn't.

'Eventually, we had to be pointed out to them so they could come and get their records signed! That's quite nice,' said Neil to the *News on Sunday*.

The judges at the Houston Film Festival appreciated the

film. *It Couldn't Happen Here* went on to win a Gold Special Jury Award. With over seventy-five entries in its category alone, the film received commendation for its 'outstanding creative excellence'. The chairman of the Houston Festival, J. Hunter Todd, said, in announcing the award, 'The audience attending the special festival première of your film was a near sell-out. The response to the film was superb and it received a fantastic outburst of applause at the end. Our jury, like the audience, was especially impressed with the exceptional choreography, music, cinematography and direction. The Pet Shop Boys themselves were superb in this unique and remarkable film.'

The most fitting epitaph is best left to Gareth Hunt, from the scene in the boarding house when he played a quite obnoxious, comic salesman. After every little stunt he would comment, 'It's only a laugh; no 'arm done.'

'It was great fun to do and it was a pity it died on its arse,' says Hunt. 'Maybe it was a little bit before its time. Anyway, Chris and Neil were two lovely and very talented lads. I think they enjoyed it as it was the first thing they had done on film.

'It was lovely being able to fiddle around with all these different, strange characters, which were made up on the spot. I must admit I liked the joke salesman for the simple reason that we did the scene in the boarding house all in one take – which was quite interesting – obviously up until when Barbara comes in and gets food thrown all over her.

'Things come out on film and you can save them, when you do them on stage, they're gone. Some stuff wasn't scripted. It just came out of the character. Like the line, "It's only a laugh; no 'arm done." That just came out. As well as the character, it became a part on the set, which was quite funny because the crew would say it.'

It was difficult filming some of the time, too, says Gareth, particularly with the elements so much against them. 'When Joss was wandering along the beach with some of the girls, and when he was on the pier, it was really bad weather. We were lucky though, because the film is beautifully shot.

Unfortunately, where it lost sight of itself was that it probably started to be a film of about twenty minutes and finished up ninety minutes in length, but Jack [Bond] does get carried away like that.

'I'm a great defender of the film and I think probably what it lacked was a good storyline. It could have been very, very good. The boys were fine, and the life about them growing up was all right, but it needed something stronger to take it through. I think they should make another one but with a definite theme through it, and include more dialogue. I would also like to see them write a film score.

'I think they are incredibly nice guys, very unassuming and very talented. They write some super stuff. I love the scene with them in the car with Joss [Ackland] and the two of them singing "You Were Always on My Mind" with Joss looking manic in the rear seat.

'I was only originally signed on to do one character and then Jack Bond gave us the opportunity to get stuck into it so everybody got a chance to play one or two parts.

'The film provided me with a great opportunity because it's not often you get the chance to play different characters that you want to on film. The ventriloquist I play was a real horrible bastard and quite frightening in a way. You think of a character like that and you think, maybe I'll tuck him away in a little folder and, who knows, at some point you might use him. It was a great opportunity to experiment, which is nice on screen. And doing something that people don't often see you do. There's something very frightening about dummies and ventriloquists, and the relationship between the two. They actually made me up to look like the dummy and it's quite frightening. Half the time you realize you are actually insulting the dummy, which was part of me as the ventriloquist. It happened a couple of times. There is a very strong bond, whether they be dummies created as bears or anything else.'

Like Barbara Windsor, Gareth would have no qualms about working with Neil and Chris again if the opportunity arose.

Neil Tennant later admitted that he thought the film was a bit impenetrable, and was, with Chris, embarrassed that so many people found fault with it. When friends began defending it, they thought they were in for some rough treatment, even if the fans enjoyed it.

The Boys were disheartened that, after promoting the film in New York, it was never shown there, although it opened in sixty-four cinemas throughout England. One of the reasons for doing the film was because they had no plans at the time to tour and, with the thought of it showing at different cinemas on a one-night-stand basis, this would make up for their lack of live appearances. Unfortunately, it was showed for longer than one night at each cinema.

According to Neil, they later felt that their big mistake was telling Jack Bond that they did not want much dialogue included.

Still, it was only a laugh. No 'arm done.

Sixteen

Season of Bad Will

Back home in Blackpool for Christmas, 1987, Chris discovered that the season of good will to all men had not filtered through to two of the North West resort's night spots. As the duo's revival of 'Always on My Mind' was being heavily featured on the playlist at Rumours fun pub and the Station Hotel, Chris and his pals set out for an evening on the town. Once in Talbot Road, Chris found he was *persona non grata*. As far as the bouncers were concerned, who refused him entry to both places because his clothes were considered unsuitable, his success was irrelevant. He was, in fact, wearing jeans. By all accounts, the doormen did not recognize the talk of the town, despite recent massive exposure over the festive period.

Like Barbara Windsor before him, Chris no doubt moaned 'What Have I Done To Deserve This?'. Bar manager Glynn Watson at Rumours explained that it was a members-only bar, and Chris was not a member. 'Chris Lowe was not dressed as he should have been. I don't see why rules should be bent for a pop star,' he said.

Ken Buckley, regional manager of Station owners Greenall Whitley, explained: 'The dress rules for the Station are no jeans and no training shoes, and they are written on external windows of the pub. We set reasonable standards which have worked well.

'The Pet Shop Boys are a very well-known group and I'm sorry it should be this way but we can't have one rule for one and a different rule for the others as it could possibly lead to a lowering of standards.'

According to Chris's mum Vivien, her son eventually ended up at the Adam and Eve, where he had a great time. While all this was going on, Neil was tucked away in a studio completing the production of a 4-track EP on ABC Records for Crazy Pink Revolvers.

Chris was no doubt delighted to learn that he and Neil began the New Year as they had ended the last – at Number One in the British charts. The beginning of 1988 indicated that the duo had kept their five-week grip with 'Always on My Mind', but were coming under intense pressure from Michael Jackson, whose third single release from his hugely successful album *Bad* had moved from Number Eight to Number Three. There was the added bonus for the Boys that readers of the *Sun* and *Daily Express* newspapers had voted them the top band of 1987, among other commendations in other categories of the polls.

It was also second time lucky for Chris and Neil when, in February, they scooped 'Best British Group' in the record industry's 1987 BPI awards. They were the only act to be nominated two years in succession. In 1987 they were pipped by the family group, Five Star. For the 1988 BPI Awards they beat Level 42, the Bee Gees and Def Leppard for the coveted top slot. Former Wham! star George Michael was voted Best Male Artist, although he missed the glittering ceremony. The newly crowned king of British pop could not attend the awards spectacle, which was televised live to 100 million TV viewers around the world. Instead, he remained in Los Angeles preparing for his world tour. Alison Moyet beat Sam Fox and Kim Wilde to top the poll in the female sector, thanks to her album *Raindancing* and single 'Love Letters'. 'Its a Sin' and *Actually* were also nominated for Best British Single and Album respectively.

During the ceremony, which was held at London's Albert Hall, the Boys performed the song 'What Have I Done To Deserve This', and were joined on stage by Dusty Springfield, whose career was re-launched with the help of Chris and Neil.

It must have been a somewhat frightening experience for Chris, decked out in the usual cap and dark glasses, to take up his position on stage, having repeatedly admitted that he hated to appear in public. A more vocal Neil Tennant was later to tell journalist Janet Street-Porter in her trendy 'Def II' BBC-2 TV series 'That Was Then . . . This Is Now', 'There aren't that many groups who have a lot to add in live performances.' He followed that segment of honest philosophy with the admission that he was bored at most concerts. 'It's kind of macho nowadays to prove you can cut it live. I quite like proving that we can't cut it live. We're a pop group, not a rock 'n' roll group,' he commented.

This diffidence and obvious dislike of anything that smacks of showbusiness is something that has characterized – and also dogged – the very private Boys throughout their career. Neil confessed that he was not overly impressed with the award. 'To an extent the award is utterly meaningless,' he said. 'It would be worth something if it was an award voted by the public. The BPI award doesn't mean to me that we are the best group in Britain'.

The Boys were upset that EMI put their Number One single, 'Always on my Mind' on a new compilation album, appearing against their wishes. During the first week of March, Neil and Chris travelled to the States where their last single 'What Have I Done To Deserve This?' reached Number Two in the singles chart. And, 21 March saw the release of another single on Parlophone from their double platinum album, *Actually*, called 'Heart'. It was backed with 'I Get Excited (You Get Excited Too)'. The record, a follow-up to their third Number One hit, 'Always on my Mind', was available on 7- and 12-inch formats. They produced both tracks with Andy Richards. The 12-inch single also featured two special extended mixes entitled 'Heart (Disco Mix)' and 'Heart (Dance Mix)', the latter having been remixed by Shep Pettibone. On 30 March, the London *Evening Standard* pointed out that the Boys had hardly struck an original note with the title 'Heart', as there had been nine Top Thirty songs with 'heart' in the title during the past twelve months, only exceeded by the use of the word 'love', which sneaked in to the Top Thirty titles thirty-two times during the same period. 'It's a real disco song,' said the Boys, 'the idea of "heartbeat", the beat of the record and the beat of your heart. It's actually pretty corny to be honest, but I think the words are quite sweet and sincere.' The accompanying video, shot on location in Yugoslavia, was a resetting of the *Dracula* story, with Ian McKellen playing the title role.

'Heart' reached the Number One slot as the Boys were holidaying in Florida. They stayed in a hotel which had been converted from an old military hospital, and which came complete with a resident ghost. Heading back to Britain, they left their single 'Heart' behind them in the charts.

There was definitely no heart behind the Boys' views on singer-turned-actress Patsy Kensit, for whom they had written and produced the single 'I'm Not Scared' for her group Eighth Wonder, released in January 1988. The Boys had offered to help the band through a dry spell, but soon regretted it. The working relationship eventually ended with Neil and Chris vowing never to work with the starlet again, apparently having been driven crazy by her childish antics. It almost reached the stage where Neil left the recording studio in anger when Patsy's boredom level hit an all-time low. Patsy admitted to the *Star* on 18 March, 'Neil wasn't happy with my attitude in the studio. I get bored while recording and I upset him by filing my nails between takes. It made a horrible noise over the speakers.

'I explained that I always file my nails when nervous and got round him by buying a dozen smoked salmon and cream cheese bagels.' She didn't get round him enough though, for, according to friends, the Boys confided: 'Never again.'

It was all so terribly different before entering the studio with the star of *Absolute Beginners* and *Lethal Weapon II*, at which time Neil had observed, 'I think she's got quite a nice voice, actually, I think she could make a very, very good record. It will be the first time we've ever done anything for anybody else; basically it will sound very much like a Pet Shop Boys record but with Patsy's vocals.

'She's very big in Italy, you know. Much bigger than us, actually. She's had a Number One and two records there, whereas the highest we've got is only Number 12.'

Neil and Chris were back in the studio working on new material in May when, for the second year running they won the 'Best International Hit of the Year' award with their own composition 'It's a Sin', a Top Five hit in twenty countries. Although expected at the Ivor Novello Awards ceremony for 1987, held at London's prestigious Grosvenor House Hotel, the Boys failed to turn up to collect their prize.

They were still closeted away on 27 June when a special limited-edition double pack was released. The package coupled their triple platinum album *Actually* with the 12-inch version of 'Always on my Mind', selling at around £7 for the album package and £12.50 for the double CD. Neil and Chris agreed with EMI's request to import quantities of the package from America when they discovered that shop-imported copies were on sale in the UK for £12 (album) and £20 (CD). The cover for the 'Always on my Mind' 12-inch was completely different from the original UK sleeve and soon became a collectors' item.

It was during April, the *Sun* reported, that the chain store, Woolworth, banned chart-busting records produced by EMI because of a row over prices. Both albums and singles from top-selling artists such as the Pet Shop Boys and Cliff Richard were stripped from the shelves until the dispute was settled. The row followed the record company's decision to cut the discount offered to retailers. EMI were not impressed that the high street giant had made the row public, as a spokesperson for Woolworths told the *Sun* on 22 April, 'We're taking this stand because we think it's unfair to pass on price increases to our customers. We'd lose thousands of pounds in sales if the dispute went on.'

As EMI wrangled with merchants, the Boys were being hotly pursued by gossip about their sexuality. As 1988 dawned, they announced that they would be backing the fight against the controversial Clause 28, which was aimed at banning local councils' promotion of homosexuality. The Boys had helped pay for an anti-Clause 28 newspaper advertisement and a spokesman told the *Daily Mirror* on 11 February, 'They support a variety of causes, and have given a lot to charity, although it's not their style to take any credit for it.' Other celebrities supporting the arts-backed campaign included Lord Olivier, Susannah York, Jane Asher and a star of BBC's 'EastEnders', Michael Cashman.

The 'gay' rumours persisted through to April when the Communards' Jimmy Somerville challenged the Boys to 'come out of the closet' and admit their homosexuality. According to the *Sun*, Neil and Chris would not be drawn. Neil said: 'We never say anything about our sex lives. It's not a clever ploy to appear mysterious. We only care about our music!'

On 5 July 1988, persuaded by Ian McKellen, the Boys appeared at London's Piccadilly Theatre for 'Before the Act', the special anti-Clause 28 show, and were the only act present from the pop world. They sang to 'One More Chance' and 'It's a Sin'. Afterwards, they said it was 'a brilliant event'.

In July the Boys became comrades-in-arms to a group of twenty Soviet schoolchildren who travelled 2000 miles from their homes in Vladimir, which lies 150 miles to the east of Moscow, on their first visit to the West. The children, aged between fourteen and seventeen, were housed in Canterbury, Kent, for a fortnight, and made history as the first Soviet schoolchildren to participate in a 'family-to-family' exchange. It was through the auspices of the *Sunday Times* newspaper that the children's dream came true. In February, the paper had followed the Soviets' counterparts, children from Canterbury's Simon Langton Grammar School, to Russia.

The Boys were as curious about the children as the children were excited to meet their pop-star heroes. As Neil told the *Sunday Times*, 'It's come as a complete surprise to us that we have any Russian following. We didn't think we were known over there.'

The children admitted that they occasionally saw clips of the duo on television, although it was nearly impossible to buy any of their records. At this time, Western LPs once having found their way into the Soviet Union, were usually copied and bootlegged as tapes.

The children jostled for autographs and posed for pictures with their stars in EMI's offices in Manchester Square, London. 'It's brilliant to meet you,' said one youngster. 'Everyone in Russia is really crazy about you.' And teenager Helena Mitina admitted, 'I won't be able to stop talking for days when I go home. I'm keeping a diary so I can tell my friends every detail. But, best of all, and they won't believe me until I show them the photographs, I'll tell them the Pet Shop Boys were brilliant.'

The Italians thought so, too, much to Neil's chagrin. The peace-loving Pet Shop Boy was mortified when he found out that football fans had adopted the duo's song 'Paninaro'. 'They call themselves the Paninaro Boys,' moaned Neil. 'The last thing I want to be is the hero of hooligans.'

The Boys kept up a hectic schedule, finding themselves in London's Abbey Road studios in St John's Wood with producers Trevor Horn and Steve Lipson to carry out some final editing on the new album, *Introspective*. The problem was that the master tape was not around. It was eventually traced to the duo's management office in Covent Garden.

The insertion of a couple of seconds of rain at the end of one of the tracks took an inordinately long time, but was eventually completed, and that same afternoon they were at Chris's North London flat ready to programme a song into his Fairlight. The song was entitled 'What Keeps Mankind Alive', by Brecht and Weill, from *The Threepenny Opera*, which the duo were set to record later that week for a programme on Radio One to commemorate the fiftieth anniversary of the opera's first performance.

The duo had trouble with Kurt Weill's complicated piano chords, but two days later, by chance, they met Richard Coles of the Communards, a classical musician. At the BBC studios in Maida Vale, he played the chords over the rhythm track. The Boys normally allow themselves a week in the studio to record one track. For 'What Keeps Mankind Alive', they had just ten hours. Proofs of the new album sleeve were delivered and Chris cast his eye over them while Neil laid down the vocals. The song, to their relief, was finished on schedule.

Thursday of that week they had to fly over to Cologne where the duo were the surprise guests at EMI's international conference. It wasn't that much of a surprise, though; half of EMI's personnel was in the departure lounge at Heathrow when Neil and Chris arrived.

Saturday saw them in Berlin for the Berolina awards ceremony – the equivalent of Britain's BPI awards. The Pet Shop Boys were to perform 'Domino Dancing' (inspired, they say, by a holiday in St Lucia, when their assistant Pete would go into a dance routine after winning at dominoes) for the first time on television; they would be miming to the track. Neil practised lip-synching from a tape in his hotel room. At the awards, the boys were announced 'International Group of the Year'. As the intro to 'Domino Dancing' swelled the auditorium, Chris dropped his portable keyboard. Never mind. The audience applauded and, having received their award from Miss Venezuela, the Boys resumed the performance with an encore of 'West End Girls'. It was enthusiastically received.

On 12 September Parlophone released 'Domino Dancing'. It was the Boys' eleventh single for the record label, and was available in 7-inch, 12-inch and cassette formats. The cassette featured a disco mix of 'Domino Dancing', plus a disco mix of 'Don Juan'. 'Don Juan' written by both Neil and Chris, had been recorded in Miami in February with producer Lewis Martinee. The Boys were joined on the track by guitarist Nestor Gomez from Miami Sound Machine, a four-piece brass section and backing vocals by the Voice in Fashion. The accompanying video was shot in Puerto Rico, and appeared with a full Latin band on BBC-TV's 'Wogan' and 'Top of the Pops'.

As autumn fell, Chris set out to make himself a splash hit in Blackpool when he told *Smash Hits* that he and Neil should make a charity record to help raise funds for the re-opening of the town's Derby Baths, which the council had decided to close. Chris explained; 'This may sound like a minor point but it's an international pool which was incredibly popular in the summer and they've got these big tubes and they're really fast – ace – and it's a brilliant building. Now it's shut because it's losing, like, two pence a year. I'm sorry but I'm absolutely furious with them.'

Chris describes Blackpool as 'a very famous seaside resort. In fact probably the best seaside resort in Britain, if not the world. Well, I'm sorry, but I've got nothing but praise for Blackpool. I love the place. You don't often realize how great somewhere is until you've lived somewhere else – every time I go back I think, *D'you know, I love this place.*' Chris says it was a good place to grow up in because it was so full of entertainment, 'I love it most at the height of the season when there's loads of drunken Glaswegians and everything, and you've got the Illuminations.'

In the same interview, Neil, somewhat tongue-in-cheek, described Chris as 'Blackpool's roving ambassador to the world. I think they should make him a free man of the city [*sic*].'

On 7 October the Boys were named alongside Bros, U2 and Sting as part of secret plans to stage a concert in aid of Hurricane Gilbert victims, titled 'Smile in Jamaica'. It was due to be screened on ITV and Channel 4 on Sunday, 16 October. And, on 12 October their new album *Introspective* was released on Parlophone, so-called because 'all the songs, although it's a dance album, are introspective.' They had considered, and subsequently dismissed, 'f', 'Dogmatic', 'Bounce' and 'Hello'. It featured six tracks and with a total running time of almost fifty minutes. The album was treated to a massive promotional campaign, with television advertisements on Channel 4, and full-colour adverts in the music Press, national newspapers and *TV Times*.

The first side of *Introspective* – which features a somewhat arty cover designed by Neil, Chris, and Mark Farrow of Three

Associates – opens with 'Left to my own Devices', a new track produced by former Buggles member, Trevor Horn, and Stephen Lipson, with an orchestral arrangement by Richard Niles. This is followed by 'I Want a Dog', which was first featured as the flipside of 'Rent'. The track was produced by Neil and Chris and was re-mixed by Frankie 'the inventor of House' Knuckles, who claimed it was almost unrecognizable from its original incarnation.

'Domino Dancing' is an extended version of the duo's Top-Ten single, at the time riding in the charts, and was again produced by Lewis Martinee. The video for the track was shot in Puerto Rico. Deemed unsuitable for UK television programming, it was instead shown on the club circuit.

The album's flipside begins with 'I'm Not Scared', the Boys' version of the track they had written for Patsy Kensit, which in fact became her first hit. Produced by the Boys and David Jacob, it features news-reel soundtracks from the Paris student riots of 1968. 'Always on my Mind' is a re-mix of their Christmas Number One single: it was produced by Julian Mendelsohn and the Boys, and mixes into 'In my House', a new title written by the Boys.

The final track is 'It's Alright', a cover version of a classic House song by Sterling Void. The Boys' version was again produced by Trevor Horn and Stephen Lipson, and features a gospel choir. The six extended tracks are faultless, high-class pop, brilliant only to the point where the very accuracy of studio-programmed sequences runs into the 12-inch, B-side extended US disco re-mix syndrome: when the yawning gaps appear. It is almost high-tech overtaken by its own dastardly cleverness.

In the shops at the same time was the Boys' first annual, *Pet Shop Boys, Actually*, which was commissioned by World Publishing and illustrated many of their 1988 events. Also included was a full discography.

On 14 November a re-mixed and edited version of 'Left to my own Devices', from *Introspective*, was released, coupled with the psychedelic 'The Sound of the Atom Splitting'. An 'exaggerated autobiography', according to Neil, the second verse refers to a time when his mother would worry about him because he'd wait in a corner of the back garden pretending to be a Roundhead soldier. Both tracks were produced by Trevor Horn and Stephen Lipson, who also re-mixed the track with Robin Hancock for the 12-inch disco single, which was released on the same day. The flipside was inspired by a passage in director Derek Jarman's film, *The Last of England*.

The Boys missed the single's release as they were on a promotional tour of America where 'Domino Dancing' was climbing the charts, and *Introspective* had just been released to critical acclaim. The album went platinum on the day of its UK release. 'Left to my own Devices' gave them their sixth Top Five hit single.

Once again, tour plans got underway, faltered and then died. 'Let's face it, we're not a band, we're a duo. And when we intepret our material, we're basically static. People accept our limitations for three minutes on "Top of the Pops", but you can hardly expect them to sit there watching us for two hours under those circumstances,' excused Neil.

Meanwhile, the Pets, according to the *Star*, were again sharpening their claws, scratching out more razor-sharp snide remarks about their contemporaries. 'As one hit record follows the next, the petulent Pets have been sneering at competition in the charts and insulting their fellow rockers,' claimed the paper. 'Pop's bad-tempered boys even poke fun at Radio One – the station that plugs their records. Vocalist Neil Tennant, thirty-three, reckons he knows more about it than most – he used to write about stars for the teen magazine *Smash Hits*.'

Neil said, 'Pop music has never been about being a musician. It's all about having good ideas – which is why videos are so important. The charts don't seem very real to me. I sometimes think we got to the top by accident, just because we sounded different.'

And if different can mean better, they were on the right track.

Above: LEAN TIMES. The Boys adapt a nonchalent pose as two of the pop world's pillars of society (*Pictorial Press*).
Below: WHAT HAVE WE DONE TO DESERVE THIS? Neil takes the mike while a bashful Chris looks on at the 1988 BPI Awards (*Rex Features*).

Left: IF LOOKS COULD KILL. Chris looks wary at a party for Eurythmics (*Rex Features*). *Below:* HELLO PLAYMATES. Neil and Chris take time out to meet Disney favourites Mickey and Minnie Mouse (*Pictorial Press*).

Left: PUTTING ON HIS TOP HAT. In his ruby-studded helmet, Chris gives the audience 'One More Chance' at the Birmingham NEC, July 1989 (*Peter Corns*). *Below:* THE QUEEN AND HER CONSORTS. The Pet Shop Boys put Dusty Springfield back on the top of the charts with 'Nothing Has Been Proved', 1989 (*Retna Pictures*).

Above: RUBBER SOULS. Chris and Neil in Michelin Man pose for an inflated shot (*Retna Pictures*). *Right:* SAN REMO STYLE. The Boys play the part at the San Remo Festival, 1987 (*Rex Features*). *Opposite page:* THE PET SHOP BOYS LIVE EXTRAVAGANZA. *Top:* City slickers out 'Shopping'. *Centre:* Neil in his 'Rented' fur coat. *Bottom:* The King and I – Neil prepares for a curtain call (*Rex Features*).

'BEING BORING' (Extended Mix)/'WE ALL FEEL BETTER IN THE DARK' (Extended Mix). Released: 12 November 1990

UK ALBUMS/CASSETTE/CD

PLEASE
Released: 24 March 1986
'TWO DIVIDED BY ZERO'
'WEST END GIRLS'
'OPPORTUNITIES (LET'S MAKE LOTS OF MONEY)'
'LOVE COMES QUICKLY'
'SUBURBIA'
'TONIGHT IS FOREVER'
'VIOLENCE'
'I WANT A LOVER'
'LATER TONIGHT'
'WHY DON'T WE LIVE TOGETHER'

DISCO
Released: 17 November 1986
'IN THE NIGHT'
'SUBURBIA'
'OPPORTUNITIES (LET'S MAKE LOTS OF MONEY)'
'PANINARO'
'LOVE COMES QUICKLY'
'WEST END GIRLS'

PET SHOP BOYS, ACTUALLY
Released: 7 September 1987
'ONE MORE CHANCE'
'SHOPPING'
'RENT'
'HIT MUSIC'
'WHAT HAVE I DONE TO DESERVE THIS?'
'IT COULDN'T HAPPEN HERE'

'IT'S A SIN'
'I WANT TO WAKE UP'
'HEART'
'KING'S CROSS'

INTROSPECTIVE
Released: 10 October 1988
'LEFT TO MY OWN DEVICES'
'I WANT A DOG'
'DOMINO DANCING'
'I'M NOT SCARED'
'ALWAYS ON MY MIND/IN MY HOUSE'
'IT'S ALRIGHT'

BEHAVIOUR
Released: 22 October 1990
'BEING BORING'
'THIS MUST BE THE PLACE I WAITED YEARS TO LEAVE'
'TO FACE THE TRUTH'
'HOW CAN YOU EXPECT TO BE TAKEN SERIOUSLY'
'ONLY THE WIND'
'MY OCTOBER SYMPHONY'
'SO HARD'
'NERVOUSLY'
'THE END OF THE WORLD'
'JEALOUSY'

'WEST END GIRLS' (Dance Mix)/'A MAN COULD GET ARRESTED'/'WEST END GIRLS' (Cat: 12R 6115). Released: 28 October 1985

'LOVE COMES QUICKLY' (Dance Mix)/'THAT'S MY IMPRESSION' (Disco Mix) (Cat: 12R 6116). Released: 3 March 1986

'OPPORTUNITIES'/'OPPORTUNITIES' (Reprise)/'OPPORTUNITIES' (Original Dance Mix)/'WAS THAT WHAT IT WAS?' (Cat: 12R 6129). Released: 19 May 1986

'SUBURBIA (The Full Horror)'/'PANINARO'/'JACK THE LAD' (Cat: 12R 6140). Released: 22 September 1986

'IT'S A SIN' (Disco Mix)/'YOU KNOW WHERE YOU WENT WRONG'/'IT'S A SIN' (7-inch) (Cat: 12R 6158). Released: 15 June 1987

'WHAT HAVE I DONE TO DESERVE THIS?' (Extended Mix)/'A NEW LIFE'/'WHAT HAVE I DONE TO DESERVE THIS?' (Disco Mix) (Cat: 12R 6163). Released: 10 August 1987

'RENT' (Extended Mix)/'RENT' (Dub)/'I WANT A DOG' (Cat: 12R 6168). Released: 12 October 1987

'ALWAYS ON MY MIND' (Extended Dance Mix)/'ALWAYS ON MY MIND'; (7-inch)/'DO I HAVE TO?' (Cat: 12R 6171). Released: 30 November 1987

'HEART' (Disco Mix)/'HEART' (Disco Mix)/'HEART' (Dance Mix/'I GET EXCITED' (Cat: 12R 6177). Released: 21 March 1988

'DOMINO DANCING' (Disco Mix)/'DON JUAN' (Disco Mix)/'DOMINO DANCING' (Alternative Mix); (Cat: 12R 6190). Released: 12 September 1988

'LEFT TO MY OWN DEVICES' (Disco Mix)/'LEFT TO MY OWN DEVICES' (7-inch Version)/'THE SOUND OF THE ATOM SPLITTING' (Cat: 12R 6198). Released: 14 November 1988

'IT'S ALRIGHT' (Extended Disco Mix)/'ONE OF THE CROWD'/'YOUR FUNNY UNCLE' (Cat: 12R 6220). Released: 26 June 1989

'DOMINO DANCING'/'DON JUAN' (Parlophone Cat: R
   6190). Released: 12 September 1988
'LEFT TO MY OWN DEVICES'/'THE SOUND OF THE
   ATOM SPLITTING' (Parlophone Cat: R 6198). Released:
   14 November 1988
'IT'S ALRIGHT'/'ONE OF THE CROWD'/'YOUR FUNNY
   UNCLE' (Parlophone Cat: R 6220). Released: 26 June
   1989
'SO HARD' (Parlophone). Released: 24 September 1990
'BEING BORING'/'WE ALL FEEL BETTER IN THE DARK'
   (Parlophone). Released: 12 November 1990

UK 10-inch Singles

(All 10-inch singles were released on Parlophone.)

'WEST END GIRLS'/'A MAN COULD GET ARRESTED'
   (Cat: 10R 6115). Released: 2 December 1985
'LOVE COMES QUICKLY' (Dance Mix) 'THAT'S MY
   IMPRESSION' (Disco Mix) (Cat: 10R 6116). Released: 24
   March 1986
'IT'S ALRIGHT' (Alternative Mix)/'IT'S ALRIGHT'
   (Extended Dance Mix) (Cat: 10R 6220). Released: 26 June
   1989

UK 12-inch Singles

(All 12-inch singles were released on Parlophone, except
where indicated.)

'WEST END GIRLS'/'PET SHOP BOYS' (Epic Records Cat:
   TA 4292). Released: April 1984
'OPPORTUNITIES' (Double Your Money Mix)/'IN THE
   NIGHT' (Extended) (Cat: 12R 6097). Released: 1 July
   1985

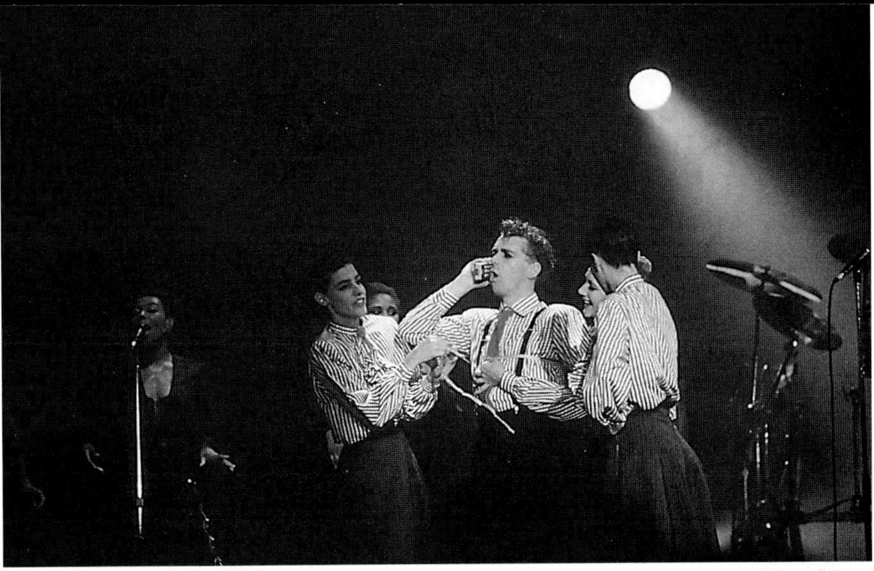

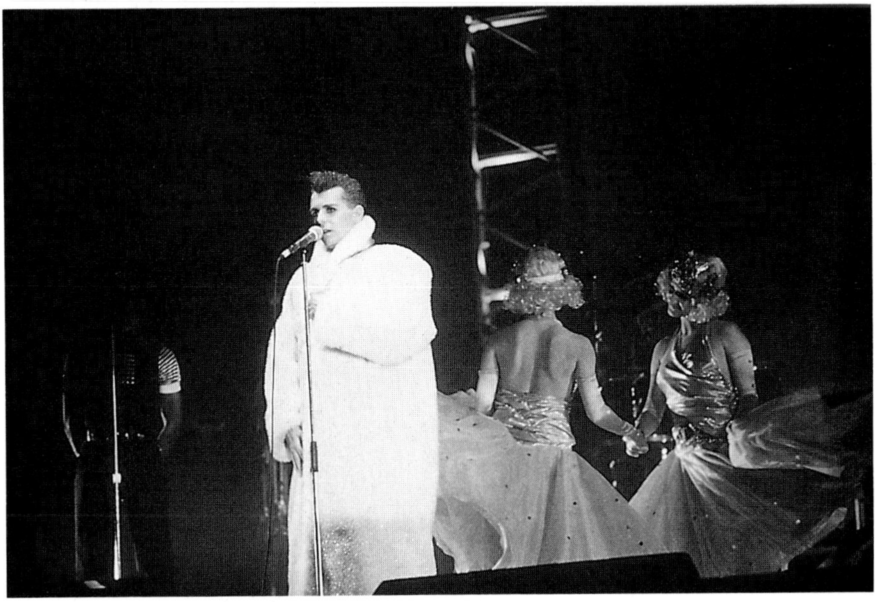

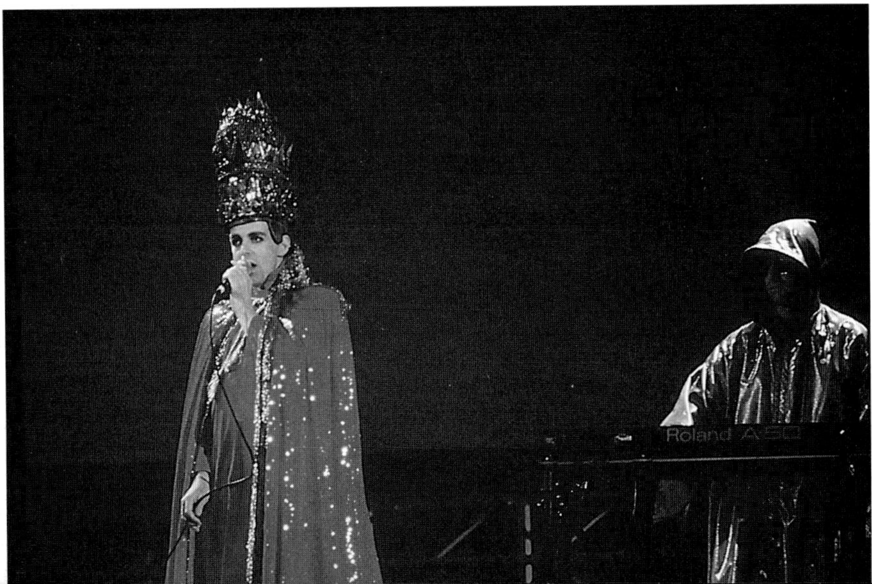
Roland A-50

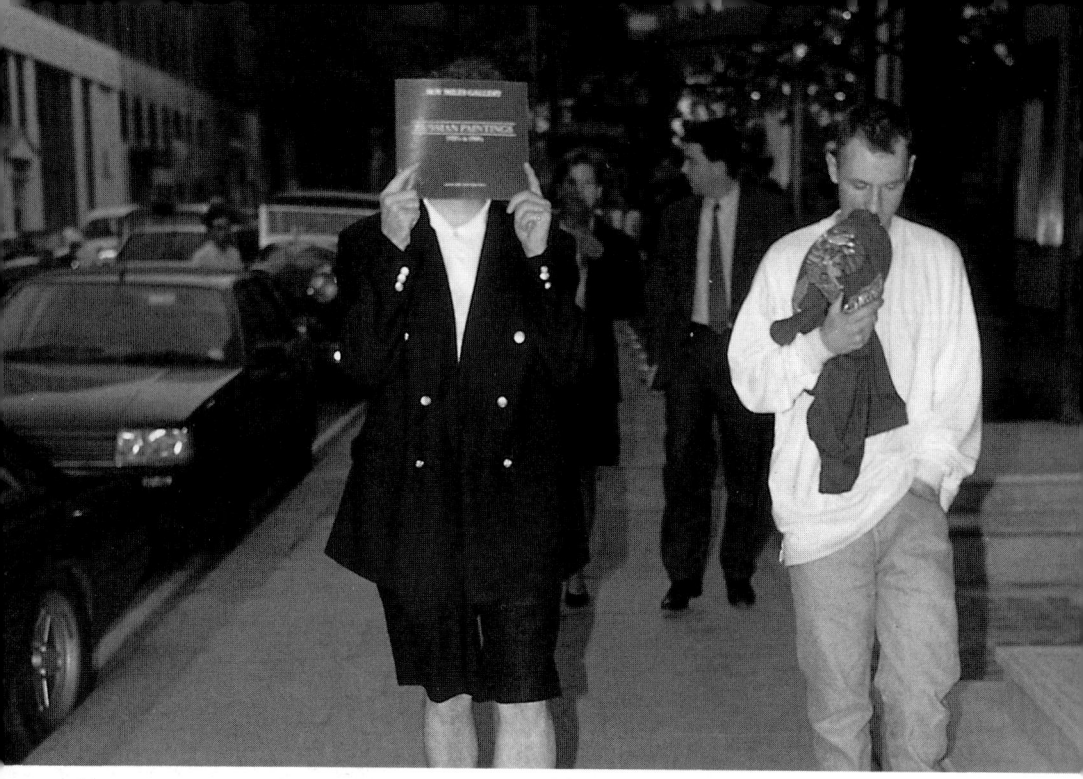

Above: NICE LEGS, SHAME ABOUT THE FACE. The Boys take steps to avoid the Press before the opening of the Roy Miles Gallery (*Rex Features*).
Below: SHADY CHARACTER. Chris keeps a weather eye open on events at the MTV awards in Los Angeles, while Neil keeps his thoughts under his hat (*Pictorial Press/Star File*).

Seventeen

Rumours and Liza Minnelli

According to Liza Minnelli, Neil Tennant always told her she was one of the original rock 'n' rollers and she didn't know it. 'It's because you wail at the world,' he said to *NME* in August of 1989.

The superstar may have been hitting the high notes with Mr Tennant, but life had not always been a cabaret for the daughter of screen legend Judy Garland. In 1984 she admitted herself to the famous Betty Ford clinic in California after finding herself on the same tragic path her mother followed. Wild nights and early mornings in clubland that she thought would ease the pressures of life had the opposite effect and there came the time when she could not stop the shaking. She had become addicted to the drug Valium – which, in fact, she had first been prescribed for her mother's funeral at the age of twenty-three – and to alcohol. The time had come for her to shed the booze and the traumatic effect it was having. 'The only thing I was looking for was relief from the pressure. You feel it'll make you feel better and it does. At first you think: Boy, Valium, what a great thing this is! My muscles don't hurt. My back stopped hurting . . . and then by that time you're addicted,' she said to the *Observer* magazine.

'Chemical dependency is a threefold thing. It's physical; it's a disease; it's definitely a medical disease. Then it is a spiritual disease and it is also an emotional thing. You can control it, like diabetics can control diabetes by taking insulin. You can control it by just not drinking.

'You see, I loved giving it up, which is very strange. But I was so relieved that there was something physically wrong with me instead of being so over-nervous I was getting crazy. I was so relieved it was something I could fix.

'Then the fun starts after that. Because without your dependency to hide behind, you begin to find out what your obsessions really are, what really makes you nervous, what really throws you, and you have to figure out what makes you obsessive.'

Liza admits that she was afraid to leave behind the record-breaking tours that were a safe and accepted way of life for her. 'But those feelings have to be accepted for exactly what they are. If somebody says something to you, just a passing remark, but it hurts you or makes you angry, intellectually you say, "That shouldn't bother me", but it does. Giving your feelings credit makes a lot of sense. Then you don't stuff them down there thinking, "I should be better than this". You're not better than your feelings – you have feelings.'

There is no doubt that just such feelings prompted Liza to follow her intuition and work with the Pet Shop Boys. She had heard the single 'Rent' and their album *Actually*, and liked the words. She found herself stimulated by the under-current beat that one could so easily dance to, and which she particularly liked, being a fan of rock music. As she says, 'They also had these almost Gregorian chant melodies and these terrific kind of cynical words.

'I spent my whole life singing songs written before I was born. Yeah! It's from growing up around them. But in my room the Everly Brothers or the Beatles or the Stones, or whoever was blasting out.

'The music I grew up with was Rogers and Hart and Gershwin; Ira Gershwin was my godfather, and I learned all the words of that era of songs as a hobby, so that when I was eleven I could tell you the verse to "Where or When" or the lyric that had been cut from "The Lady Is a Tramp". But I loved to dance to rock and move around to it. I loved Dylan and stuff like that, but I don't think I had the nerve up until now to do it.

'You know, it's been safe. You do something, people like it, they know what to expect and you do it well; that's terrific, and if you're not careful you could stay there. But you get to a point where you're willing to take the risk of people throwing rocks, 'cause you gotta do it.'

The Boys, it seems, never felt inferior or overshadowed by this superstar of stage and screen. 'They've always just treated me like I was a singer. They've managed to ignore all the crap that goes along with being famous, I guess.'

Neil has told friends, 'Liza is fabulous, but the thing about Liza is that she is fabulous all the time.'

The opportunity for the Boys and Liza to work together occurred quite by chance. Liza was in her record company offices at the same time as Tom Watkins. She mentioned that her favourite track by the Boys was 'Rent', and enquired whether she could record it. Watkins, ever the opportunist, suggested that she should get Neil and Chris to produce a couple of the tracks on her forthcoming album. It was after they met that the Boys said they wanted to take on the whole of the production.

'I went to a lot of friends when I started this project and all of them thought that it was a wonderful idea to work with Neil and Chris,' says Liza. 'I mentioned it to Cyndi Lauper, who's a wonderful writer and she's got great instincts, and she said, "Yeah, it sounds terrific!". And Michael Jackson liked the idea a lot. Joan Jett I talked to, and Elton [John] and Rod Stewart. Y'know, just people that I've known and worked with throughout the years. I feel like I'm dropping names and I don't want to. But doing the job I do, those are the sorts of people I mix with,' she told *Smash Hits*.

The Boys were delighted with the opportunity before them. Says Neil, 'When I first came to London, 1972 or 1973, I was a big David Bowie fan and Liza Minnelli was part of that scene – David Bowie, Roxy Music and the film *Cabaret* all seemed to be part of the same thing, divine decadence or something. I thought she was a very glamorous figure.

'Also, she hadn't made a proper pop record or dance record, so that was interesting, it was like she was a totally new artist. And, also meeting her she had no preconceptions, she wanted to make a record that was avant-garde by her standards. We have no interest in making a middle-of-the-road record, we basically made a Pet Shop Boys album and Liza Minnelli sings it.

'Somebody interviewed her and said, "The Pet Shops have written and produced this record, what do you do on the album?". And she said, "Well, I sing it, you know, all the vocals are by me". It pisses me off that for some people that's not enough.'

The Boys approached the album like they would any of their own, which this was, in a sense. They propped up standardized disco pop with neat lyrics and tuneful hooklines. Included on *Results* was a version of the Tanita Tikaram melody 'Twist in my Sobriety', 'Rent', the lustful 'I Want You Now' and 'I Can't Say Goodnight'. All the material was chosen by Neil and Chris.

Neil was given the tape of Tanita Tikaram material by a friend in the press office of Warner Brothers when she signed to the record company. Neil thought the track 'Twist in my Sobriety' was fantastic. 'This was just before we were approached with this Liza Minnelli project, and I was trying to get Barbara Cherone [Warner's press office] to get Warner's to stop Tanita Tikaram recording it for her album. I was saying, 'Listen, never mind her, she'll probably never happen anyway, get Liza Minnelli to sing it and she'll make some money.'

'Liza was crazy about it, she particularly liked it because it was about sobriety and she's famous for having had a drink problem many years ago. She really, really wanted it to be a statement, you know.'

'Says Liza, 'What I always look for in a song is the lyrical content. I'm never going to sing a song about just anything. I can't do it. That's where I would feel I was compromising if I had to sing *"la nee nah nee nah, let's dance, let's not dance"*. Why? Gimme some lyrics, I'm fine.'

Tanita Tikaram later told me, 'It was a real compliment to have Neil Tennant choose one of my songs and it was very adventurous of Liza to use the song in a manner that was so different from her usual style. I think she deserves a lot of respect for the whole project.'

If anything, the Boys worked Liza hard in the studio and weren't afraid to pull her up if they thought she was approaching the lyrics from a wrong angle. 'They really pushed me, they really made me work. On this song called "Love Pains", I was singing, *"luuuuvre pains"*, and I heard this tapping. Neil looked at me and said, "Why are you singing *luuuuvre*?" I said I thought I was supposed to. He said, "No, sing it the way you normally sing it . . . sing it like it was Charles Aznavour.'

Of the album, Neil says, 'A lot of it is quite sexy. That's the way she sings; but also, she acts the songs. She'll describe to you what the person looks like that she's being in the song. Which is quite unusual. She sounds very convincing; you don't think, Oh, Wow, this is Liza Minnelli singing a Pet Shop Boys song. She hasn't had to compromise and we haven't either.'

Many saw the collaboration as a strange mix – the hi-NRG, Euro-beat kings and the classic cabaret star. There were hints of campness behind it all, something that annoyed Neil intensely. 'I always maintain that we're completely misunderstood anyway, but people often say, it's wonderful, it's so camp, and I just smile politely because I'm a bit disappointed, really, because it wasn't meant to be camp.

'Actually, real camp is when something is totally sincere, and Liza Minnelli has one hundred per cent sincerity in what she does. There is no cynicism or trying to be clever. It's a fantastic quality, that. You can see it in her eyes when she sings straight at you in the studio.'

According to journalist Andrew Billen of the *Observer*

magazine, 'They [Pet Shop Boys] enjoy a gay club popularity partly because their records resemble the best of the Euro-disco played in gay discos and partly because they burlesque the genre. As long ago as Christmas 1986 *New Musical Express* was abusing them for not coming out of the closet, missing the point that the Pet Shop Boys are not a gay band but a camp one that thrives on the suggestiveness of songs like "A Man Could Get Arrested".'

When Billen put the camp connection to Liza, she reeled, 'God, I never thought of that. I don't think so at all. It's none of my business what these guys do in bed but what they do in the studio is phenomenal and they're complete gentlemen and I'm very close to both of them. They've never been offensive or overtly strange to me. I never even thought of that.'

Like everything else in her life, Liza took the recording in her stride, although she admits to not knowing what a 12-inch single was at the time, or re-mixes in the studio: 'That first time I met Neil and Chris I came in ready to meet the musicians and they said, "There are no musicians." There were just these machines. . . .'

Results was an encouraging departure for her. 'I'd wanted to make a rock record all the time but I was frightened of taking the risk. It's hard to be disliked or unaccepted. And I've never been good when people get mad at me, but I've come to a point in life when I'm willing to take the risks I've always wanted to.'

So much so that Liza found herself face to face with the camera crew on 'Top of the Pops'. 'The thrilling thing is, every show like "Wogan" . . . if you have a big film or a stage show, you would still do those shows, but you would only do "Top of the Pops" if you had a hit. That's what was so terrific about it.

'Neil came down, because I was terrified – I was in shock – and he said, "Don't smile." I asked, "Why?" and he said, "Why smile? You're doing this for yourself, not anyone else, it's rock 'n' roll." So I didn't smile when I was on and after I said to Neil, "but everyone else was smiling. . . ."'

Asked what she thought of working with Chris, Liza was complimentary, 'Chris's attitude is so great. 'He's so fearless. You say, "Do you think it's wrong to do this?" and he'll say, "Who's to say it's wrong, let's do it."

'It's really just thrilling when you're sharing all this with people that you care about. This record . . . it doesn't sound like any record I've heard. I want to do more stuff like this. Especially with them.'

Jon Homer, writing for *What's on in London*, would not recommend such a quick reunion, judging by his review of *Results*. 'The importance of the producer in selling records and, sometimes, selling the artist, should not be underestimated. So the bright spark who came up with the idea of pairing Liza Minnelli with Neil Tennant and Chris Lowe, aka the Pet Shop Boys, was obviously hoping that the pop duo could do for Minnelli what they've done for Dusty Springfield. Unfortunately they haven't and *Results* is one mess of an album.

'Here Minnelli murders the Pet Shop Boys' "Rent" and slaughters Tanita Tikaram's "Twist in my Sobriety", which for some reason starts with the thudding drum sound that inspires so many hi-NRG records, totally inappropriate to the song and not nearly as outrageous as somebody obviously thought it was.

'Indeed Minnelli doesn't handle the bulk of the material on *Results* awfully well. Only on the Sondheim-penned "Losing my Mind" (Sondheim-penned it might be, but naff song it is, too) and on the lushly orchestrated "Love Pains" does she manage to invest any real sense of passion or power into what is an extremely mundane record.'

Neil's former employer *Smash Hits* gave it six and a half out of ten score, as Ian Crenna noted, 'Although there are at least two more deservedly huge 'n' tuneful hits here, namely the brilliantly catchy disco of "Love Pains" and the gorgeous fake seventies soul ballad "I Can't Say Goodnight", the big disappointment is how very predictable most of this is . . . mostly this sounds like the usual Pet Shop Boys ingredients slightly reshuffled. As for Liza, her husky actressy manner doesn't really suit the bustling drum machines and synthesizers much of the time and comes a poor second to Neil Tennant's affecting melancholy sincerity.'

Record Mirror said that, ' "Twist in my Sobriety" refused to take the route one expected, thumping where it was expected to glide and putting the brakes on when it looked like it might take to its heels.' The album, said Johnny Dee, took amazingly ambitious turns, and was as much an adventure for Minnelli as it was for the Pet Shop Boys. '*Results* is a massive record that contains just about everything you could ever want from a pop LP combined with Liza's refusal to wear a leather skirt and do a Bonnie Tyler impression. The greatest triumph is the least rock 'n' roll moment imaginable. A lush symphony lays a bed of roses for Liza's heart-wrenching rendition of "Rent", proving just how good that song is.'

Sounds pointed out that the much-touted collaboration was not as crazy as it might have at first appeared. Wrote Peter Kane: 'There's always been more than a touch of the camp, theatrical, grand gesture to Pet Shop Boys and Minnelli is certainly enough of a trooper to turn on the necessary technique for a show-stopping item like "Losing my Mind" or "Don't Drop Bombs". We'll perhaps draw a discreet veil over the clanging, wash 'n' brush up given to Tanita Tikaram's "Twist in my Sobriety". Yet, there's a more predictable choice of covers for the Boys' own swooning "Tonight is Forever" and the marvellous "Rent" which comes complete with a massive orchestra and a whole new meaning. Even when this is bad, it's almost good. And that, as they say, is entertainment.'

Eighteen

A Life on the Open Road

Despite the success of their work with Liza Minnelli later in the year, 1989 had not got off to a very auspicious start. By all accounts comedian Jimmy Tarbuck snubbed the Boys by refusing to star in their planned new video. The idea was to include Tarbuck's gushing introduction of their television spot on 'Saturday Night Live at the Palladium', but the comedian, who had hosted the show, said, 'I'm not getting involved with those miserable blokes.' Apparently Tarby, as he is affectionately known in the business, had not been impressed when Neil refused to wave to the audience at the end of their television performance with the Liverpool-born comic.

Said Neil, 'It was over a silly thing about us waving at the end of our bit in the show. We said we couldn't wave and that was that.' A spokesman for Tarby said, 'I'm sure there was more to it than whether they waved.' Neil's last retort was, 'He said we were miserable bastards, so we couldn't have it. I was quite proud.'

A week later, the Boys collected a top music award before a 7000-strong crowd at the World DJ-Mixing Championships at London's Royal Albert Hall. It also featured Yazz, Sheena Easton and Alexander O'Neal.

At least they had the satisfaction of looking towards their much-awaited tour. The bashful Boys who had refused to perform live for their fans because they thought they would look too boring, suddenly announced that all was to change. An offer from a Japanese promoter named Mr Udo had prompted them to move on apace from those early junior disco appearances and prove to the waiting world what they could really do.

In the past, they had blamed their decision on lack of finances. This time it was feasible. 'We want it to be spectacular, involving members of the English National Opera Company and a full dance troupe. It could set us back around £500,000 and right now we don't have that kind of money,' Chris Lowe had stated previously.

Now all was about to change; as Neil pointed out at the time, 'It's taken a lot of heart-searching, but we've finally decided to take the plunge and play live. The main problem we face is that we're a duo and when we interpret our material we are basically static.

'So it's a bit much to expect fans to sit watching us perform for an hour like we do for three minutes on "Top of the Pops". But we're getting round that by signing up a full dance troupe and members of the English National Opera to give value for money.

'We'll be able to provide a really good show for our fans. They're entitled to it after all they've done for us.'

Promoter Andrew Bull announced live dates for Hong Kong, to begin on 28 June, followed by five dates in Japan and a trio of bookings in Britain – at the Birmingham National Exhibition Centre on 15 July, Glasgow SEC on 17 July and London's Wembley Arena two days later.

The shows were to be directed by Derek Jarman – who first met the Boys when they asked him to direct the video for 'It's a Sin' – the film-maker whose most recent theatrical production was *L'Inspirazione*, by Sylvano Busotti, at the Florence Opera House in 1988. Directing a pop show on this scale was to be a new experience for Jarman. He said, 'I have done everything else I've ever wanted to do. If I had the chance to live my life over again I wouldn't change a single thing,' he said.

For the Pet Shop Boys' spectacular, Jarman was to make forty-five minutes of a new film, to be projected on screen.

Christopher Hobbs, whose screen designs included Jarman's *Caravaggio*, Ken Russell's *Gothic* and Neil Jordan's *Company of Wolves*, was brought in as production designer. The theatrical concept held great appeal for Jarman. A strong believer that pop music is in itself theatre, it was not hard for him to link the two art forms.

'They asked for a theatrical concert and that's what we're doing,' he said. 'I suppose some people think pop music and theatre shouldn't mix, but I think pop music is theatre, and I don't see why it shouldn't be so. To my mind, there're two ways of doing it – you either just sit there and sing on a stool and do it the simple way, or you go for it.'

Unlike the three-minute promos the public have grown used to from other pop quarters, Jarman videos – The Smiths' 'The Queen is Dead'; Marianne Faithfull's 'Broken English' – have been built on a tradition of mini-films. Wembley was to be yet a further extension of his directing abilities. The film backdrop he was designing would be 'much more cinematic than a pop video. It's visual rather than narrative, running parallel to the songs. The surprise will be in the fact that the film is seventy mm – no one's used that as a back projection in pop concerts before,' he told *City Limits*.

The film, the Boys, the music, lighting, dancers, musicians, would all be integrated, the film being half of the performance. The idea was not to illustrate the songs, but to run parallel with them, as a backdrop. It would be brighter, bigger and clearer, and a considerable improvement on other such backdrops. The Boys wanted something theatrical, and he was not going to disappoint them.

Jarman found it easy to conjure up images for the songs after closely collaborating with Neil and Chris. He found them good to work with, and felt under no pressure as a filmmaker. They were happy not to interfere, leaving the film side to the professional. 'Neil says he's sometimes insecure but he strikes me as being clear thinking,' says Jarman.

He found them very modern, contemporary in their outlook,

and he liked the way they made their music. The songs, he says, are wonderful to dance to, with a liberating quality.

Several leading names in the musical world had been approached to flank the Boys on stage. There was legendary saxophonist Courtney Pine, percussionist Danny Cummings and keyboard player/programmer Pete Gleadalls, and an extra keyboard player, Dominic Clarke.

A troupe of dancers – Casper, Cooley, Hugo Hulzar, Tracy Langran, Jill Robertson and Robert Lamorte – was also involved, and began rehearsals in Los Angeles with choreographer Casper Canidate, who had been involved in the 'Left to my Own Devices' video, and whose work could most recently be seen in the video for Michael Jackson's 'Smooth Criminal'. Backing singers were Carroll Thompson, Juliet Roberts, Mike Henry and Jay Henry. The make-up artist was Pierre La Roche.

Neil went to great lengths to explain to the Press and public alike that the Pet Shop Boys were not a rock 'n' roll band, and therefore the shows would take on a completely different slant to the Bon Jovi-, Def Leppard-type shows of this world. It was important to the Boys that their audiences knew what to expect to avoid the disappointment of not finding the cliché rock 'n' roll concert scores.

'This is the tour we have waited three years to do, in terms of presentation and production,' enthused the Boys.

Rehearsals were held at the West London Nomis studio complex. The *Guardian*'s Mark Cooper called in on the Boys and, like most people, was totally unprepared for the uncharacteristic smile on the face of Chris Lowe, who greeted the journalist.

With the array of instruments before him, including those of fellow musicians for the tour, Chris admitted, 'It's almost like being in a real group. Actually, there's really no need for me to play anything. I might as well have programmed it all, but I'd probably get tired of dancing for the whole show.'

Dancing?

Of the setting, Chris explained, 'We wanted an empty stage

because we wanted a theatrical production where the making of the music wasn't paramount. We're not great fans of live music; it's great when the group comes on, the entrance is always terribly exciting and then, with a few exceptions, things tend to get terribly boring.'

Neil believes the only point in seeing someone play live is to see a virtuoso like Prince or Stevie Wonder. 'Our claim to fame is not being virtuosos but being songwriters and being the Pet Shop Boys. There'd be no point in us trying to do a traditional rock 'n' roll show. One of the main reasons we've never toured before is because to do it our way, you've got to try and persuade everybody in advance that our way makes sense.

'It's difficult to get people to understand how un-rock 'n' roll this show is going to be. In the Sixties, you'd have called it a multi-media happening or a spectacle. We've taken the songs as a basis of a visual presentation of which the elements are the Pet Shop Boys and their musicians, a troupe of dancers and film, lighting, costumes.

'One of the other reasons for doing the show like this is what we regard as our limitations as performers. We always think you could do a cartoon of the Pet Shop Boys in which I'd be very tall and stiff and . . . bossy, and then Chris would always be bouncing along behind me like one of those Fanta ads.

'You do get people who want to expose themselves totally to the public. That's why we work with them, because they're fascinating and totally unlike us. With Liza [Minnelli], there's no gap between her public and her private life. In fact, you feel like you're on stage when you're with her. Liza Minnelli is simply Liza Minnelli.'

On the other hand, Chris says they have always imagined the group as something different to themselves as people.

Neil has always had a penchant for musicals – having taken part in them at school – and show-stopping numbers. 'I've always wanted to do something in that vein rather than a rock show, which never really interested me. I remember watching the Beatles as a child and thinking how awful they sounded. They used to go on and I'd be going, "God, they don't sound a bit like the record." You used to be a bit terrified and think, Oh God, they're really hopeless. What you want is people to be even more so – like the record, only better.'

After abandoning the Europe and American tour announced in 1986 because of the prohibitive cost of staging such elaborately planned shows in small venues, their only true "live" sets throughout their career were at the Brixton Fridge in 1984 when they used backing tapes for six songs; in 1985 at the ICA; on BBC2's 'Whistle Test' the following year; on the televised American MTV awards in 1986; and, in 1988, at Before the Act, an Anti-Clause 28 benefit at London's Piccadilly Theatre.

The projected American tour in 1986 had even reached the ticketing stage, with seven nights sold out in a matter of three hours. 'Even at that time our basic idea was that we were going to have a director and that what you were going to see was not a spontaneous rock 'n' roll concert – which generally involves the performers in the role of virtuosos. There's no point in, say, Eric Clapton doing a theatrical show, because you go to see him being a virtuoso guitarist. But the Pet Shop Boys, neither of us could be called virtuosos,' says Neil.

'Our starting point was, "What would we like to see if we were in the audience?" So we got involved with two guys from the English National Opera to help devise a show – actually we got involved with a lot of people. When we did the Clause 28 benefit, which was directed by Richard Eyre of the National Theatre, he came up to us and said, "I was going to direct your first concert." And I'd probably forgotten that before we got involved with the ENO guys, there'd been a possibility of working with him, too.'

In 1987, they had shelved a second tour due to studio commitments. Neil says that one of the reasons the duo had been able to maintain their fresh approach, continue to enjoy themselves, create new ideas and write new material was because they had not undertaken any gruelling tour schedules. The one they had planned for this year was perfect, with five dates in the Far East and seven in Britain.

At the turn of the year their management company, Massive, had brought in Ivan Kushlick, a veteran of the touring scene who had previously worked with Def Leppard and Sade, two extremes if ever there were any. Neil admits, 'Previously our management had very little idea how to take a group on to the road.' Suddenly there were no excuses. Lowe kept telling Kushlick there was no way the duo would be going on tour – that was until the Japanese promoter fronted enough cash to finance the dates in Nagoya, Osaka and Tokyo. Several months later, two dates were fixed for Hong Kong and seven in Britain.

Says Neil, 'We felt a bit sneaky, going off to the Far East and missing out on home.' Once it had been decided, however, it didn't take very long to get everything up and running.

They had their hands full in the studio working on the Liza Minnelli album, as well as being involved in the tour. Fortunately, most of their music is already sequenced and can quite easily be transferred by media information to their stage equipment through a processing operation. The song list and running order was apparently selected in just two hours at Neil's flat.

At the same time, the Boys saw Derek Jarman's film of the Benjamin Britten War Requiem and had decided to ask him whether he would be interested in directing the show.

Jarman had a film library from which he could draw. As it transpired, most of the footage he ended up using for the concert was new. For example, he shot the sequences for 'King's Cross' as soon as he heard the Boys were going to do it. 'He was on the phone to us the next day, telling us he'd already done it. He worked in Super-8, which is very flexible – and it keeps the cost down,' said Neil.

The bulk of the studio work was completed by the end of April, but it was only on their arrival in Hong Kong on 26 June – and only three days before the tour was due to open – that the show was finally rehearsed on a full-sized stage. The

Boys had held a dress rehearsal at Brixton Academy prior to their departure.

The fact that, upon their arrival, the locals were declaring that the Pet Shop Boys were the second only to Madonna in the colony could not have helped their nerves or feelings of apprehension as the big day approached. Two days prior to the first show, at a Press conference staged at the Ramada Renaissance Hotel, Neil admitted that he had only begun singing with the duo as a holding operation. At one stage they had considered approaching Jimmy Somerville, but changed their minds. A singer by default, Neil admitted that he had never liked his voice, but once they started recording it was too late to introduce another vocalist.

Their main worry in Hong Kong was that one of the computers might fail – always a possibility in these circumstances. They had a back-up system, just in case, but if it needed to be employed it would have been a question of stopping the track and beginning all over again. Relying on a computer bank to generate the music obviously carried its own headaches, although Chris enthused about the live sound.

Jon Wall, writing for *Time Out* magazine, was at the first show in Hong Kong – which was far from sold out, and at which the Boys arrived on stage twenty-five minutes late. Wall said the sound was predictably, gut-bustingly loud and metronomic. On some occasions the songs sounded so much like the recordings that a check was necessary – it was apparent that they were live, however, whenever Neil reached the limits of his register and things became just a trifle strained.

Coolness is the purpose, aloofness their trademark, he wrote.

The duo began with 'One More Chance', Lowe in leathers and crash helmet, Tennant in sparkling PVC against a Metropolis background. 'Opportunities' featured the first of Jarman's surreal Super-8 footage. Early high spots were apparently an exuburent rendering of 'Heart', and 'Paninaro', which saw Lowe doing a spot of desultory hoofing, while two knife-slashing women fought it out on the wide screen and three dancers enacted a *Romeo and Juliet* scenario beside him. The most exceptional song was 'It's a Sin', which followed an intermission of programmed sound and synthesized lights. 'A *tour de force*,' wrote Wall, 'the song comes in like Hell according to Hieronymous Bosch and goes out like the last half-hour of *Raiders of the Lost Ark*. Tennant, dressed in a violent red cape, brandishes a trident, while on screen behind him, Jarman attempts a five-minute re-make of *Sodom and Gomorrah*.'

During rehearsals the Hong Kong censors had objected to part of the film that accompanied 'It's a Sin', particularly during the scene for 'Lust', where two boys are seen to be kissing. They agreed that the projectionist would cover these portions of the film with his hand – fractionally too late on the night, although no more was said on the matter.

The censors also objected to the word 'Fuck', which appeared during the song 'Nothing Has Been Proved', from the film *Scandal*, about the Profumo affair. Images appear on stage, super-imposed with words and phrases. Neil and Chris had objected to this in the first instance, but for some reason it had remained as part of the imagery. As a result, at the correct moment, the projectionist was instructed to black out the word.

Says Neil, 'From the outset we decided that if we were going to play live it was going to have to be different, to be theatrical. At the time, nobody was doing that kind of thing, not even Prince or Bowie. And, for a while, whenever people asked us whether we were going to tour, for some reason we found ourselves saying yes.'

According to Chris, their reluctance to tour was never as simple, nor as clear cut, as they enjoyed making out. 'The reasons why we didn't play live had nothing to do with nerves, pressure or anything like that, but everything to do with the kind of show we wanted to put on.

'At the time everyone was playing Wembley Arena for five

nights, doing exactly the same sort of show – even down to using the same backing musicians and vocalists. It was becoming so boring that once you got there you might just as well have headed straight for the bar and stayed there for the rest of the evening.'

So had all the pre-planning, the drama, the tension, been worth it for that Hong Kong debut, which, in fact, went off without any major hitches?

'Yes, I think we were both very happy because it's such a complicated show for us to do. I suppose we felt elated and relieved,' admitted Neil. 'Often when you do something you have all these fantastic ideas, and by the time you realize them, they always end up getting a bit watered down. In this show, nothing has been watered down. The only thing that hasn't happened is that Chris wanted to ride a motorbike on to the stage. It would have been good, but it was too much, really.'

Chris did, however, admit that he would have liked Hong Kong to have been the only venue. 'I'd prefer it to be a one-off; we have to do it again now,' he mused at the time.

Back at their hotel to celebrate the first night, amongst the messages and presents they discovered champagne from their management stable pals Bros. Chris's card said from 'Watt and Luke'! Neil was on a high, grandly claiming to journalist friend Chris Heath that it was one of the most spectacular shows that had ever been done in terms of pop music.

Any minor hiccoughs had been ironed out for the following night's performance, although the projectionist continually annoyed the promoter by forgetting to censor part of the 'It's a Sin' film. A percussion solo by Danny Cummings had been added between songs, giving Neil time to get changed before 'Domino Dancing'.

Neil missed his entrance after his quick change from striped shirt for 'Shopping' into an embroidered one for 'Domino Dancing' became a slow change – then he came in at the wrong place. Chaos prevailed. Fortunately, Courtney Pine stepped into the breech and in-filled with a semi-instrumental while Neil pondered his next move from the side of the stage.

'It was exciting. I rather enjoyed the disaster,' he told *Smash Hits*.

The Boys remained a contradiction in terms after the Hong Kong shows, undecided half the time whether or not they enjoyed it. They claimed to *Smash Hits* that 'not only have we done a live show which sounds good and everything, but it's also one of the most spectacular shows that has ever been done in pop music', then Neil would claim that being on stage was not all that rock 'n' roll legend claimed it to be. 'I had to keep thinking, "concentrate", because I start to drift off and think about what we're having for dinner.'

Even so, Hong Kong proved a good starting point for the tour. Most British and American acts who play there are considered to be boring – they simply stand and sing – as opposed to locally popular artists who employ troupes of dancers and undergo various outlandish costume changes. What 7000 people at the Coliseum witnessed on the Pet Shop Boys' first-ever live concert was something from their own back yard, with a sixteen-song set, a troupe of dancers, Jarman's film footage, and major costume changes to boot.

Three weeks prior to the first show, a new three-track single was released. 'It's Alright', the classic by Chicago House artist Sterling Void, which the Boys had recorded for their *Introspective* album, was re-recorded with producer Trevor Horn in a new pop version with additional lyrics from Neil about the threat facing the world environment. 'It's about the power of music', says Neil. 'It's a bit cosmic really – it's saying that if people still make music then there's always going to be a good side to what people do, so mankind is never going to be totally destructive. It's very sincere and there's something about the song that makes perfect sense . . . music is an inspiration to people and always has been an inspiration to people. Music represents the good side of mankind; music tends to be a good force rather than a bad force.' Two new Tennant/Lowe compositions also included were 'One of the Crowd', featuring Chris on lead vocals, and 'Your Funny Uncle'. The single was released on 7-inch (three tracks), extended disco 12-inch (three tracks), cassette single (three tracks) and 4-track CD. DJ International in Chicago also prepared a re-mix of the Boys' version of 'It's Alright' with Sterling Void.

The *Sun* thought the song was a big yawn. 'Have you noticed that several international superstars have got really boring lately? Take the Pet Shop Boys with "It's Alright". It isn't! They whine away with pretentious lyrics about world disasters but say music will go on and on. Not music like this, I hope. They are perfectly capable of making interesting records – "Always on my Mind" was brilliant and "West End Girls" was clever. But this dirge could send listeners into a coma. Better luck next time, Petties.'

If the reviews disappointed the Boys, it was nothing to what happened during the filming of the video to accompany the single. For stylish Neil was forced to discard his favourite leather jacket after the filming. He had forked out £6000 to be a dad for a day to 110 babies, but the experience went horribly wrong when Neil attempted to cradle one of the tiny tots. She promptly threw up her lunch over his £800 designer jacket.

The Boys had recruited 'every professional baby in London' for the video shoot and paid parents £50 each to let their babies appear in front of the cameras. A startled Neil could only gasp when the baby vomited, while Chris and the camera crew fell about laughing. 'He was speechless at first. It was so funny to see his expression. But he soon saw the amusing side and creased up with laughter,' said one of the insiders.

'I certainly got the baby bug after being surrounded for a whole day by wet nappies and crying babies,' said Neil to the *Star*. 'We had veterans of more than one hundred nappy adverts. I enjoyed it so much I now want one of my own. The video features them scratching their noses and smiling. The new single's about the future of the world and I thought it was best to use babies instead of making a political video.'

Up and down the country, Pet Shop Boys fever was growing. Fans scrambled for tickets. Two nights at Birmingham were quickly sold out and a third was added, and one night at Wembley Arena had extended to three.

The Boys had also decided it was time to set up an official fan club. Since 'West End Girls' in 1986 they had financed a free information service for fans, but the volume of mail had increased so much that they could no longer operate on their own. Part of the new service was to include a magazine, to be produced three times annually, and called *Pet Shop Boys – Actually*.

'The problem was that we didn't want to charge people but the whole thing got out of control so we decided to freeze the whole thing. Then we decided to start a paying fan club where people get three magazines a year. I think people are actually dissatisfied getting things for no money – they want to be sold things. We are charging £10 a year and we're making no money from it,' says Neil. For your tenner you also get two glossy photographs, a poster, and a key ring.

In charge of the fan club is Mike Hrano, who also runs clubs for Chris de Burgh, the Godfathers, the Christians and Bros. 'The Pet Shop Boys turned it down at first because they had such a low opinion of fan clubs,' he told the London *Evening Standard*.

Neil was forced to celebrate his thirty-fifth birthday party in Siberia. He popped the corks whilst flying back to Britain after the Japanese dates. To accompany the bubbly, a stewardess presented him with two birthday cakes.

Back on terra firma, Neil said of the tour many claimed would never happen here in Britain, 'It'll be totally different. We think most live concerts are a bit boring really. I don't go to many now. I only go if I know I'm going to like it. Like Prince. And Brother Beyond were good too – he's a good singer. My favourite concerts are where people scream.'

He qualified that by commenting, 'Oh no, I don't want to be screamed at', to *Number One*.

'We always knew that if we toured we would want to do something different. We wanted to add to the original songs, but what actually changed our minds was a purely financial thing. People think that when you're a pop star you've got limitless money, but it isn't so. We got a really good offer to play in Japan and we thought it was a bit sneaky just to go and play there and not play England. We didn't want to have sponsorship. Actually we have got some sponsorship in Japan, but that's only on the back of the programme.'

Neil admitted to leaving nothing to chance, particularly down to the way they dressed for the stage. He had brought in numerous expensive costumes – and even splashed out £7000 on special 'Acid House Anoraks' for the roadies.

With regard to who they considered their audience, Neil said, 'I don't mind having a mixed audience. A lot of groups complain about having a teenage audience, but we love it. Young fans are the most interesting. I always like the people who are enthusiastic about things. Young fans are so honest. They tell you if they think you're rubbish in a video.'

They didn't get what they had hoped for, as the Stud Brothers pointed out in *Melody Maker*: 'The audience was a disaster. Where are the children? we thought. Pop should have children. Tennant knows that. Pop should have screaming, sweaty, salty children; gorgeous, gullible, monied children. And we just couldn't see any. It is difficult to spot anybody under twenty-five and almost impossible to spot someone who didn't look like they sell things. The men wore Farrah slacks, ginger suntans and white leather shoes and the women (lemon minis, frazzled peroxide perms and white leather shoes) looked like the sort of women who're pregnant at fourteen, married at sixteen and never get to enjoy a kiss, let alone pop. These are the people who listen to Simply Red. They're not the Pet Shop Boys' audience.

'But they are. It's a disgrace. Our ideal Pet Shop Boys audience consists of thousands of Euro-kids, a couple of hundred T'd gayboys from Troll and maybe a few of those weird twenty-five-year-old anorexic women who fall in love with you and threaten suicide. They're the reason Tennant and Lowe chose Derek Jarman to direct shows. It had nothing to do with this bunch of wankers.'

It seems the dimming of the lights thankfully relieved the Stud Brothers of this unsightly mob and instead were treated to what, to them, seemed like several years of the Balanescu String Quartet.

Well, the Boys had planned to be different, and they were. They about-turned conventional rock concerts on their heads. Members of the Balanescu Quartet attempted to soothe an indifferent Birmingham audience with some of their classical repertoire. It fell embarrassingly flat. It was definitely not what they had come to see.

'If you're the Pet Shop Boys there are two good reasons to be supported by a string quartet. The first and most obvious is the camp value, the second, probably unintentional, is that if the only witnesses to your scrambling of aesthetics think of aesthetics as some kind of pulmonary disorder and jeer at it, you're almost guaranteed an ecstatic welcome.

'And it was an ecstatic welcome. Sadly, not the kind of ecstasy we prefer, not the shrill shriek, pitched in orgasm, but a great macho bellow, a terrace camaraderie. We imagine if any of these people were ever to actually meet Tennant they'd slap him on the back, thrust him a pint of light and bitter and call him Nazza. Ugh!' observed the Stud Brothers.

The Quartet was followed by six dancers dressed in black PVC macs, which they stripped off to reveal grey PVC suits. There was Neil in a grey longcoat, and Chris behind racks of synthesizers sporting a glittering red motorbike helmet.

Jarman had admitted that he did not like going to concerts because he hated the crowds. He needn't have worried. Empty seats went begging the first night at the NEC due to the concert being tacked on to the front of the British itinerary by the over-enthusiastic promoter. A curtain had even had to be erected to partition off the empty back half of the venue.

Tim de Lisle observed in the *Daily Telegraph*, 'On television Neil Tennant, the thirty-five-year-old singer, has all the charisma of a weatherman but moves around less. Chris Lowe, the morose synthesizer-tinkler, makes Tennant look like James Brown.

'With all this detachment goes a tendency – anyway, on record – to hedonism, to gay abandon. On stage, they made a bold attempt to have it both ways: while the two of them remained doggedly inert, Derek Jarman was brought in to get every sort of theatrics going on around them, with the help of six dancers, four throaty backing singers, a giant video screen and even two real musicians (including Courtney Pine on saxophone). Tennant entered into the spirit of things sartorially and ended up prising the Birmingham All-Comers' Record for Costume Changes from the grasp of Diana Ross (seven costumes to six).

'For a band which likes to be different, there is a lot of dry ice about and one or two of Courtney Pine's contributions are the pneumatic equivalent of the lengthy guitar solos purveyed by the sort of groups the Pet Shop Boys disapprove of; but these are peripheral matters – all you need is stage presence and Tennant, with his tentative walk, nasal voice and endearing stiffness, hasn't got it. You can see why they used not to want to play live, though you have to hand it to them for trying,' observed Tim de Lisle.

Neil had declared on the eve of their debut concert tour, 'Sometimes we've been puzzled as to what the entire point of playing live is, anyway.'

David Sinclair in the *Times* replied that part of the idea was for the musicians to reveal something of themselves to the audience through the performance of their art, to make flesh and blood that which otherwise exists only as a series of electronically coded and stored impulses.

'But Tennant, who wandered through a succession of daft costume changes looking like a waxwork version of the comedian Julian Clary, and his utterly impassive keyboard-playing partner Chris Lowe, evinced stage personalities that were as engaging as a blank sheet of paper,' wrote Sinclair.

The Jarman back projections, he said, were bold, if crass, illustrations of the song lyrics. 'The limitations of Tennant's glum, adenoidal voice were badly exposed on 'You Were Always on my Mind' and 'Left to my Own Devices', but the four backing singers put in a tremendous effort, and there were other visual diversions in the shapely forms of a six-person dance troupe. Courtney Pine, who received a rapturous ovation, lent the music some gravity with one or two ostentatiously virtuoso solos, but was otherwise boxed into a tight corner by the unsupple, metronomic rhythms of the backing tracks. There was a human percussionist, Danny Cummings, but his embellishments were subsumed under the rigid, impersonal sound of the computer-generated disco drum tracks.'

There was a disconcerting hollowness at the centres of the performance, said Sinclair, which even the pithiest material, like 'Heart', 'Rent' and 'Shopping' could not conceal. This, despite the memorable pop soundtrack the Boys had provided the Eighties with, and one that had reflected both the glamour and the hardness of the era.

Only the majestic version of 'It's a Sin' lifted the evening momentarily for Sinclair: 'Tennant, dressed at this point in a long red robe and wearing a king's crown which would have given Elton John a headache, was flanked by dancers dressed as grotesqueries (a pig, a witch, a gross John Bull), while the back projection was taken up with mildly risqué shots of sensuous-looking young men. For a moment the aloof façade slipped and he sounded as if he meant what he was singing. Normal service was, unfortunately, quickly resumed.'

Love them or loathe them, the Pet Shop Boys cannot be ignored, and *Hello* was certainly on their side. The live experience was definitely worth waiting for, it said, the performance at Birmingham NEC and Wembley Arena possibly being labelled the year's leading roadshows from a variety point of view. This was a fair observation, as there had indeed been plenty of variety in the guise of videos and theatrical costume changes. Neil's quick-change antics had found a fan.

'Most of the songs were presented as mini-plays or musicals, reminiscent of Kate Bush's one and only stunning tour ten years ago,' said *Hello*. '"Rent" was like a bizarre version of the Black and White Minstrel Show and almost as surreal as the boy's much-maligned feature film, *It Couldn't Happen Here*. They sang all their hits, but the highlight was "It's a Sin", for which half of the players were decked out as the seven deadly sins – to the audience's delight.

'Musically the Pet Shop Boys' synthesizers made them sound almost identical to their records – but when you've produced some of the most successful pop since ABBA, this can be overlooked.

'Despite this lack of "live" sound the concert managed to create an exciting atmosphere of controlled energy. Plus this was more than just a concert; it was pantomime, charades, fantasy, music, mystery and imagination all woven into one. Or to paraphrase one of the Pet Shop Boys' best tunes, "*Che Guevara and Debussy to a disco beat*".'

For many of the audience, it was hard to decide whether to concentrate on the pouting, immovable Tennant, and the sullen-looking Lowe, or Jarman's sixteen films that accompanied the songs. Tennant did nothing to alter his normal, stilted stance, apart from undergoing various costume changes. The famous nasal whine was ever present. Yet, as the Stud Brothers were right to observe, when Tennant stepped back from front stage and did more of absolutely nothing, he did it with such awesome, unreasonable panache, that the audience was blissfully uncaring of the rampantly ridiculous theatrics of the dance troupe.

The highs were high and the lows were a definite disappointment to the fans and the simply curious. 'We knew that the Pet Shop Boys could never, ever have been as great as everyone claims because pop isn't like that. Pop exists in cathode rays and on the covers of glossy magazines. Tennant knows that. It should only ever be part of the dream factory. The moment it takes to the stage, no matter how big, it looks smaller than a copy of *Smash Hits*,' the Stud Brothers observed wryly.

'Pet Shop Boys came as close to unreal as you can be in the flesh. They were almost other-worldly. They tried and we liked them. We liked them a lot. But we liked them a lot where previously we had loved them. They could never have been unreal enough. Simply good.'

Journalist Paul Mathur of *Melody Maker* loved the show, drawing parallels between Tennant and Lowe and *Star Wars'* R2D2 and C3PO, wandering wide-eyed around a surrealist future world of their own making. The Pet Shop Boys, he said, made soundtracks for their own existence. They had set out to destroy any assumptions about what a rock performance entailed, the show being closer to theatre than pop, their rationale being to create a spectacle riveting enough to draw attention away from the core personae of Tennant and partner Lowe.

'At their best – "Rent", "Love Comes Quickly" and particularly the deadpan "Paninaro" – the Pet Shop Boys magnificently re-invent Vegas showbusiness in a contemporary style,' noted Paul Mathur. 'It could have fallen apart, but by the time the credits rolled on the giant screen it had been a glorious success. The Pet Shop Boys are truly the first postmodernist pop stars, drawing ahead of their peers with every step. Astounding.'

Whether the assembled crowds saw it that way was a matter of opinion.

In the past, Bobby Orlando certainly had not wanted them to go live the way they eventually did on their tour: 'I saw them on TV in America when "West End Girls" was a hit here in 1985 and they were horrible. It was ridiculous. Neil was up there and he was really stiff, and very nervous, and he looked intimidated. He was wearing this cowboy hat that was too big. Chris was not his usual jovial, bubbly self. I remember at the time I was talking to them about if they were going to go live, that the way it should be done was with a proper band, and the band should be stark, and almost look like British skinheads. They shouldn't be pretty boys with the little hair-dos. When I say British skinheads I don't mean evil and mean looking; they should look like a British boxer would look.

'I almost thought of Neil and Chris like Ron and Russell out of Sparks. The keyboard player was great with his little

Hitler moustache and he sat there, real stiff, and made eye movements. The other was a cute little guy running around the stage, and it worked. They were one of the classic pop groups that should have been huge but weren't. I envisioned Neil and Chris being that kind of a thing with normal-looking musicians in the back. But they were not interested in going live at that time.'

The Boys were in fact rebelling against traditional live sounds like the guitar, an instrument which Chris, in particular, loathed. On 'West End Girls' there was a classical guitar piece at the end that, for this very reason, was played on an emulator.

While they were with Orlando, they didn't even want the big theatrical production. They were going to be strictly a recording group that would branch out into production at some point.

'The problems of going live with the kind of productions that I understand they have been doing is, how can you make any money? When I heard about the tour I thought they had probably got a good pay day out of it and that they were probably just exploring something they wanted to try', notes Bobby O. 'But I didn't think it would be long lived because it is not their personality. I'm not surprised it didn't last. Going on the road and touring is a hippy mentality; it's communal living. The Allman Brothers and the Grateful Dead could tour forever because that is the way they live.

'The Pet Shop Boys would have died a death in America. Bowie tried something like that recently and it hurt his career. You are talking about a bunch of housewives from New Jersey who may come in and see theatre, but kids who buy Pet Shop Boys records aren't going to want to see that kind of thing.

'Right now the only thing the Pet Shop Boys have to do here [America] is have a hit record, or they should just drop out and never make another record again.

'The producers they work with don't add anything to what they are doing. I am not saying they subtract from it. Neil and

Chris were never near the place when we did the mixes. They pretty much left it to us, and we never let them down. They were always happy with the stuff we did.'

During August, the first single from the Boys' collaboration with Liza Minnelli, a hi-NRG version of Stephen Sondheim's 'Losing My Mind' was released, and proved to be her first hit single, justifying her faith in their expertise . . . 'I just put it [the album, *Results*] completely in their hands – the ultimate trust. It's weird, because I've been working for thirty years, and to find somebody who you like enough and trust enough and respect enough to say, "forget it, I'll do whatever you want" is quite amazing.'

The Boys were back in the high life again in September at the prestigious Society of Composers, Authors and Publishers' annual awards show in London, where they were due to perform. Chris Lowe suddenly made his excuses and left, to perform elsewhere. Colleagues and the hosts were concerned about the sudden disappearance, and they were right to be. Chris had apparently gone to the lavatory, but he never came back. Head down and avoiding any eye contact, he hurried away from the event and disappeared into the night.

A month later came the first announcement that the Boys and Tom Watkins, the man who had so brilliantly steered their career since they first signed with Parlophone in 1986, would be parting company.

On 20 November, the Dusty Springfield single, 'In Private' was released. At Christmas, the 'Splash' column of the *Star*, with a little help from the readers, named the names who had helped to shape the Eighties. A national poll was organised to establish the most popular stars of the decade. Duran Duran swept the board for best group of the past ten years, closely followed by U2 and the Pet Shop Boys. That wasn't all. In the Top Twenty listings, 'Always on my Mind' was voted in at Number 17. Band Aid's 'Do They Know It's Christmas?' was the top single, followed by 'Relax', by Frankie Goes to Hollywood.

For the Pets, it had been a year when they were finally

prepared to shed their aloofness and expose their obvious vulnerability to the pressures of live work. The waxen images so often personified on video had melted away. Not many critics warmed to the metamorphosis; some hardly noticed any change. Yet, the Boys maintained their dignity throughout. For those who had caught the duo live, it was a rare glimpse of self-presentation running hand in hand with self-preservation. They had albeit been forced into a corner and had to go live to prove themselves once and for all to a frustrated fan base and a Press all too ready to cut them to pieces. They were two Pet puppets who were working their own strings – ready for people to cut them down to size. And was this to be a dummy run? Could we expect more from them? They wouldn't say. The saga of designer detachment was to continue.

The previous Christmas, manager Tom Watkins had treated both the Boys and Bros, whom he was also managing, to tickets for the *'Allo, 'Allo* theatre show in London. The night Neil and Chris turned up, half the audience were more interested in wriggling in their seats to catch a better glimpse of the Boys. At the NEC Birmingham, Glasgow, and Wembley Arena, some of the audience were no doubt wriggling in their seats for a different reason. Still, it was all for the sake of pop art.

Nineteen

The Piglets of the Eighties

'One of the clever things about their whole image is that they have managed to retain a cult status in the States without ever losing their image, without selling out, and yet they have also had some huge hits; it's a very difficult combination. Most people can't manage that at all,' says Jonathan King. 'They manage it partly because of the fact that they don't perform, or they haven't really performed, and therefore the performance side of things has not been there to let people know that they are a serious, real band, so they have become a cult thing. Yet, on the other hand, the records have been strong enough to turn into consistent hits as opposed to one-shot hits, which those sort of cult bands would normally have.

'Let's face it, they really are the piglets of the Eighties. What I was in the Seventies, they are of the Eighties. They have done that very cleverly. I don't know whether that's down to them or to Tom [Watkins]. I have a suspicion it's probably them. Artists who have too much control over their own careers can have problems sometimes. But, on the other hand, it can work if you have got the brains, and they obviously have.'

Jonathan King first met Neil Tennant when Tennant and Lowe received the award for best single of the year with 'West End Girls' in 1986, when King was hosting the BRITS awards. 'I couldn't remember having met the Boys until we were all on the same aeroplane going over to America. We chatted and got on famously. I thought they were great fun and had a lovely sense of humour. They were very clued in, knew what they were doing and where they were going. They seem to be pretty on top of it all.'

King attended their Wembley concert, in which he said there were flashes of brilliance on stage, in particular 'It's a Sin' – one of the greatest things he had seen in years – and huge patches where all it needed was for somebody to sit them down and say, 'Hold on a moment, edit this, change that.' As King says, that is sometimes indicative of a talent having too much control over themselves.

'My problem with the McCartney concert, for example, was that obviously McCartney has nobody who says to him, "Look, we've got to change this, we've got to change that", because they daren't speak to him. When people get to be quite big stars people are frightened to speak to them. I don't know whether that is what has happened with the Pet Shop Boys but definitely if I had been part of the management team, I would have taken Neil and Chris to one side and said, "This show is shaping up brilliantly in some areas, but there are other areas where there are huge patches."

'They had the laser thing which worked well for about twenty seconds, but it went on for about two minutes, obviously in order to give a break in between the songs. Therefore, it went from being a clever idea to being a rather irritating idea, to being incredibly boring, to being absolutely infuriating by the time they came back. Now it doesn't need a genius to know that that's going to happen and say, "We've got to turn that down, so if we need that length of time longer we have got to put something else in there."'

'As for playing live, he [Tennant] had the same problem that I had. Neil knew that really he was a behind-the-scenes person. I never did go live, that's why I had all my disguises; that's why I became Shag and the Weathermen and everything else. I was also extremely competent, as he is, at making hit singles. My problem was, I wasn't prepared to go live because I knew it wasn't really my scene, and as a result I never really sold any albums, so actually the money I made from the business came very rarely from my own work, much more from the work of others who I then nurtured and developed.

'Looking back, I made a serious mistake. I should have gone live. Not for the ego reasons of being a star, which I was always happy not to be and am still happy not to be, but for the sensible reasons that Stock, Aitken and Waterman watching my progress discovered, and they have often said to me that their great people who they watched and followed were Motown and myself. And what they did was, they learnt from my mistakes. They obviously saw what I was doing and said, "These are Jonathan's pluses; this is why he has all these hits but this is where he is making serious mistakes and he is not building any artists and he is not making any money."

'I think I should have gone live. I think the Pet Shop Boys were right to go live. It was the right decision to make. They very nearly did it terribly well. There was enough very clever ideas in there for it to work. Neil has got the brains to be able to be aware of the fact that he can do a perfectly good live show because he has got enough great tracks with guest artists to perform them. A lot of them would be happy to pop along. To put together something almost like a variety show.

'Just like I should have probably gone out and had long stretches of time when I was doing monologues or dialogues with the audience, answering questions back and playing on the controversial side of my character, and having video screens with me saying outrageous things on television. Perhaps putting together a show which also didn't rely on the fact that I was staggeringly good looking and could stand on stage and do a wonderful show, or even like the Phil Collins approach of being just a really great musician and doing it so well on stage.

'The trick is, if you are going to go live and you are like the Petties are and like I was, don't fool yourself into thinking that you are something you are not, which they obviously haven't done. Quite clearly Neil knows exactly what he is and what he and they can do.

'The mistake is thinking you are someone like Wham! and going out and trying to do that, and you end up looking stupid. Neil is too intelligent to do that. He is dead right to have done what he has done live. If he is going to do it this way, which is make the Pet Shop Boys into an act, sell Pet Shop Boys albums, he has to go out and perform to people on some level. It can be a very limited level, but they were right to do it.

'Bits of the concert were some of the best on-stage things I have ever seen. As a whole it didn't really work for me because there were too many other bits that I didn't enjoy. People who went probably enjoyed it because of all the songs. It was far from a failure. I would say it was generally a success but a rather qualified success.

'We have this problem in the UK that the media like to rip everything to shreds. I find things change. I will think somebody is wonderful, tell everyone they are wonderful, rave about them, then a few months later watch them go off, or just go off them myself.

'I loved Melanie when I first heard her. That little-girl voice. After about a year it got excruciatingly irritating. It was nothing that she did. It was that I had heard it enough and it was no longer original or clever, it was just irritating. I think the rest of the world felt the same and she sank without trace. Things like that can happen.

'The Petties have done very well and I don't think they have a bad image in Britain. Their problem is developing now to the next stage, which is obviously what they have taken time off to do. I very much wanted them on the BRITS show [1990]. They came back with the answer that they really were doing nothing and intentionally doing nothing, but would be delighted to be on the 1991 show if they are still around, which was probably the right answer for them career-wise. It meant them not burning any bridges.

'I would usually advise artists intent on taking time off not to do it quite that radically, like Level 42 with their eighteen months off. I would suggest they make a single six months or nine months in and keep things bubbling. Level 42 are more of an artist but less commercially successful. They have probably got their artistic loyalty base to a greater degree, although they are not real artists that can take two years off like an AC/DC or an Iron Maiden.

'It's wise for the Petties to give it a bit of a rest. They haven't dried up completely because there has been the Liza and Dusty material. They decided to make a management change with Tom which meant radical re-structuring and working out how things go. If they have got sense they will be doing exactly what I said they ought to do and that's find somebody who can give them good advice, which I suspect they probably will.

'When I met Neil I thought his head was pretty much screwed on. We had the same sense of humour. For a start he can laugh at himself.

'Why the split with Tom Watkins? Tom was a man of great flair – but not their style. The best way was to terminate on an amicable level and find somebody who was a little less flamboyant and inspiring, and more down-to-earth, together, and plodding, even. Neil's probably looking for a team of people who are almost like accountants and lawyers to handle that side of things and what he needs is a Tom Watkins-type character to bounce his ideas off, which is probably one of the reasons why he has retained his friendship with Tom and is using it at that level.'

King believes the duo are popular in the States because they make extraordinarily good pop records when they make the right ones. They have made six or seven classic, great pop records and they always sell and the Americans are very good at marketing those – much better than we are actually in Britain, he says. If they see something that's really good commercial talent, it's out there and is sold like crazy.

'When a band have six or seven major hit singles in the States and, yet, are not out there on tour, they are going to develop a little bit of a quirky image. The Pet Shop Boys, like They Might Be Giants, are a bit bizarre to the Americans. They are a bit odd and not entirely what they ought to be. On that level they are appealing as well as being highly commercial. That is why they have managed to hit the underground market as well as the overground one.'

King suspects Neil Tennant is the brains behind it all, the one with the great ideas. 'They are very much poised on the edge of a precipice, but also the edge of a mountain. If that is the problem, and they are not taking advice from people who they respect, then they are probably finished. Because that is indicative of it going to their heads, which it didn't seem to have done when I met them.

'But you never can tell these things, in which case they will have more and more control over what they do. What tends to happen then is the flashes of brilliance slacken off and the vast amount of not being quite so good keeps going on. And each of the people who said to them, "Hold on fellas, you are making a mistake here", they are not listening to. And when they put out a record that isn't really good enough, nobody has the guts to say, "Neil, this is rubbish, don't do it."

'I would think that Neil desperately needs somebody who is on the same wavelength as he is and therefore can praise him with his great ideas and encourage his flashes of genius, but also very cleverly put him off making mistakes. I think from looking at the whole Pet Shop Boys, that is what I have always felt about them. They have genius inside them but they also have the seeds of destruction and it all depends on whether or not he finds some people to give him that right advice. I say he because it struck me that Neil is probably the dominant part. He has the ingredients of two things – one, to continue to make as many hits as he wants for as long as he wants, but two, of being a marvellous person for our industry.

'He's the sort of person who, when we are both in our eighties, could well be sitting down gossiping over the last half-century of the music industry that we have both been a part of.

'I would suspect that Neil has found that the industry is actually a wonderful and fascinating place, which it is. I am a great person for defending our industry . . . It has been wonderful to me over the last quarter of a century, and I don't see any reason why it shouldn't be wonderful to him, and I think he has discovered that. He knows there is a great lot of fun to be had. If he develops rightly he will stay in it and he will be marvellous in it. If not, God knows what will happen.'

A hit master himself, King is the key position to judge the Pets' steps to stardom. And if he agrees they're stepped correctly, he's not the only one. Their break from the pop scene left a multitude of fans waiting with bated breath. They didn't wait long. The Pets were back with their best . . . and they were on their best behaviour.

Twenty

Memories Are Made of This

'There is no pay-back time,' stresses Bobby Orlando. 'I have done well with the Pet Shop Boys. There were a few things that they had written that always clarified my position. The only comment I always felt and the only frustration I ever had throughout my whole relationship with them was the fact that they ended up on EMI, which I always found to be incredible because they had passed on the group. If they had wound up on any other label it probably would not have been as frustrating.

'I felt very paternal about Neil and Chris. I felt compelled to protect them – to look after them and guide them. To protect them from the cruel and evil music business and the demons that are employed by that business. In a sense, I wanted to protect them from the cruel and evil world. But I discovered that they really did not want or need my protection. Somehow we perceive as frail and breakable the things we care so much about when in reality these things are quite strong and unbreakable. We always end up losing the things we strive to keep yet we can never rid ourselves of the things which we try to abandon. That's why people are never really happy and most certainly never fully content, regardless of their station in life.

Bobby has received many offers – including one from a film company in Germany – to buy out his entire master catalogue, which is extensive, with Divine, the Flirts, the Pet Shop Boys, and Lisa Lisa. Frankly, he doesn't need the money. Right now the catalogue is his link to the music business. It would be at least a year before he would sell them off to another company.

Whether he becomes involved in the music business in a year is going to depend largely upon what kind of artists are out there. If what's out there today is going to be out there in a year, then that's it for him; there is nothing out there that is attractive to him.

What attracts Bobby Orlando are several Pet Shop Boys songs he retained that were very important because he recognized them as great tracks. (When the duo settled with Bobby Orlando, they relinquished all further royalties on his versions.) Of course, the Pet Shop Boys can re-record any of the material in Bobby's care, but, more importantly, they cannot restrain him from putting material out. The reason he hasn't put new material out in the past year and a half is because he has been waiting for them to come out with their new album first. He says, 'Right now, to be honest, if I put out these numbers I don't know whether it would mean anything. They have to re-build or re-structure something. And then, of course, I am going to try to profit from it as best I can. By taking time off, I don't know if what they did was smart or stupid. I think it was stupid.'

They also had another song called 'To Speak Is a Sin', also recorded by Bobby Orlando. It is one that he gave them back and one which, he says, they should release. 'I wish I still had it,' he says. 'Another they have which is fabulous is called 'Pet Shop Boys' [the song that the *Smash Hits* team in London were most impressed by]. It has never been released because I own it. I didn't release it because it didn't feature enough of them. It is a twenty-eight-minute piece, like a concerto, with all classical piano. It is unusual and very abstract. Some parts are disco, others break-dancing, with different rhythms and patterns, yet it is one continual flow of music.'

Bobby has fond memories of his time with the Boys, and is upset when he thinks about the problems that arose when they finally left Bobcat. 'I did what I had to do legally, and it was a matter of three days, not a year. There was no lawsuit.

It was quick and done. They had these lawyers who were telling them the contract was bullshit, so I had to attack the lawyers.

He says it is sad the way Neil and Chris interpreted events.

'I called them to tell them I didn't like their last album but I did that as a friend and as a producer. They could do much better. There were one or two good songs on it, but they are capable of making records like "It's a Sin".'

The hip-hop dance world that they were initially exposed to thought they were wonderful. Radio was also attracted to them. They were taken up really quickly, at a time when Bobby himself was peaking as a producer, and he had done some of the best stuff of his career at that point.

'Prior to making a penny with the Pet Shop Boys, obviously it had cost me a lot of money,' he says. 'Chris Lowe and Neil Tennant are exactly fifty/fifty input into that duo. Neil could not be the Pet Shop Boys without Chris, and vice versa. The only reason Neil might be a little more in the driver's seat is because he is the singer and the voice is more identifiable than a keyboard player – particularly one who doesn't play! Even if Chris just plonked a chord or two, it was the way he played the chord. And he played it differently. He would play an A-minor chord differently to the next person. We would do it the correct way, he would do it the incorrect way and his way would sound better. He didn't care at all about me playing. He thought it was funny.

'Now if they are smart they will make 'Bobby O'-sounding records. I'm not saying that from an egotistical point of view. They will make the kind of records that made them successful. If they are foolish they will keep making 'Domino Dancing'-type stupid records that make no sense for them to do. Any success they have as a result of those records, should be used to make an important statement. They should not release another record unless they have somebody listen to it after it is completed, to review it. They need someone, whether it is myself or someone like myself who really knows what they are doing. They should heed the advice I gave them then and they should heed it today. It is more true today than it was then.

'You have to focus on whatever you want to do in your life. From 1980 to 1987 I had one goal and one goal only – to be the McDonalds of the record business. I wanted to release more records, like they release hamburgers, than anybody could have. I didn't care if they sold or if they didn't sell. I wanted to be a part of the Bobby O story and when 1987 came and I had finally reached that goal and my company released over one thousand records I said, "That's it. No more".'

By then Bobby had sold off a good part of his company. He wrote a book that he had been working on for three years called *Darwin Destroyed*, which refutes the theory of evolution. The book was a key turning point in what Bobby wanted to do with his own life. He sent the Boys a copy of the book. They never responded.

'At that time the book was my tunnel vision, and then I was going to decide what I wanted to do for the Nineties. Now [1990] I am really one year away from making the final thrust into what I am going to do with my life,' he says.

Prior to entering the music industry, Bobby had attended pre-law school. Now back with his studies, he plans on taking the Bar exam in summer 1991. He is also a registered lobbyist.

'If there is going to be any kind of continuance in the music industry for me, it's going to be in such a way that it cleanses the industry. Right now it's run essentially like a large mafia. It's like a big conspiracy, with a unit of power brokers that rule the industry. I think I could best do that in a legal capacity or in my lobbyist capacity.

'The Pet Shop Boys for me wasn't just another record ultimately. Maybe at that point I was trying to cleanse the system and I was using them as the mop and they didn't want to be the mop. The Pet Shop Boys were my rainmaker and the fact that that rainmaker didn't happen to me was really perhaps God's way of saying, "That is just not the environment that I want you to be in". Consequently, I have never got excited about another artist I worked with after that.'

Bobby O has neither produced nor released a new record in two years.

Twenty-One

Here We Go Round Again

On 4 December 1989, a single called 'Getting Away With It' was released. It was by a group called Electronic, formed by Bernard Sumner of New Order, and the guitarist Johnny Marr (of the Smiths). The public were surprised to see a familiar face on the video for the song – that of Neil Tennant. He had, in fact, co-written the song and also sung on the record. Neil's involvement had come about after a mutual friend relayed a message earlier in the year that he would like to be involved. The song reached Number 12 in the UK charts.

As the New Year dawned, it was all change for Neil and Chris. Having left Massive Management on good terms, the Boys established their own office in London's Notting Hill Gate and employed Jill Wall – formerly with Parlophone Records and Polydor Records – to run it on their behalf.

In April, they flew to Germany and headed for studios in Munich to begin work on their next album, with producer Harold Faltermeyer. They had been offered the soundtrack for the film of Fay Weldon's *The Life and Loves of a She-Devil*, which was to star Meryl Streep and Rosanne Barr, but they decided to concentrate on their own album, instead.

On 4 August, the Pet Shop Boys made their first live appearance in America, when they guested on two songs performed by Electronic at the Los Angeles Dodgers Stadium, in support of headlining act Depeche Mode. The same performance was repeated the following night.

The first single off the new album *Behaviour* was released on 24 September. Called 'So Hard', it was, according to the

Boys, about 'two people living together. They are totally unfaithful to each other but they both pretend they are faithful and then catch each other out.' It entered the UK chart at Number Four.

Smash Hits placed it in their 'Single of the Fortnight' slot, opening with: 'You can just tell a Number One as soon as you hear it, can't you?' Hinting that it would have made a better instrumental, reviewer MC Tunes commented: 'I think he's got a great voice, but it's better suited to ballads. I mean, when I hear the name Pet Shop Boys, it suggests to me middle-aged people listening to their CDs in their nice homes and I think his voice makes it sound middle-aged. It would have been a great sort of House record for kids if it was an instrumental.'

Record Mirror's review of the extended dance mix version said, '. . . Harold Faltermeyer co-produced, Julian Mendelsohn mixed, bleepingly introed then dated late-Seventies-style Kraftwerk/Giorgio Moroder-ish electro-driven rattling twittery pulser is lispingly groaned as usual, with an even stronger more solidly electro instrumental Dub Mix flip.'

The album *Behaviour* followed on 22 October, featuring ten new tracks and including musical contributions from Johnny Marr, with orchestral arrangements by Angelo Badalementi – the man who became a household name through his atmospheric musical score for the hit television soap 'Twin Peaks'. The strings of the Balancescu Quartet – who were support act on the Boys' 1989 UK tour – are featured on one track.

Chris told journalist Stuart Maconie that he hoped the album – which entered the British charts at Number Two – was less digital. 'We wanted to get away a bit from samplers and pre-sets just so that we didn't end up sounding like everybody else's records. We went and worked with Harold Faltermeyer 'cause we knew he was pretty good at twiddling the knobs and doing "real" stuff. He went out and bought all these first generation clumsy synthesizers. We still couldn't resist using all our favourite samplers, though, but perhaps it's a bit richer, more warm and human . . .'

Critic Roger Morton of *New Musical Express* said that three years on from the epic blue House exhilaration of *Introspective*, and while dance culture had blossomed, the Pet Shop Boys 'appear to have been at the pruning shears. In its subject matter – loneliness, deceit, loss, nostalgia, the delusions of fame – *Behaviour* is probably no more a disconsolate record than *Introspective* or *Actually*, but what's been snipped away at is the consoling omni-presence of a defiant surge of rhythm.

'The grandeur and uplift of the past has been replaced by a pervasive mood of pondering sadly. And, (perhaps) unpardonably in a duo who have staunchly defended the potency of teen music and the desirability of an audience of screaming girls, *Behaviour* is inescapably laden with a particularly thirtysomething variety of wistfulness. The smell of defeat, not wet knickers.'

Twelfth November saw the release of the single 'Being Boring'/'We all Feel Better in the Dark'. The flipside, produced by the Boys, featured Chris on vocals. In an interview with *Smash Hits*, Neil was quick to explain that 'Being Boring' was all about not being boring! Asked whether they worried that the public might be getting bored with them after five years, Neil commented, 'We are quite pessimistic people. We always run everything on the assumption that it'll all be over tomorrow. I suppose we do worry a bit but it's not a huge paranoia. It's a boring thing to say this but if you make records that you think are really good it would be very frustrating if they weren't a success. At the end of the day you'd probably think that the public was wrong.'

As one of four partners in the Decorative Arts Group, Neil, with Johnny Marr, attended the opening in Manchester of an exhibition by Central Station Design (responsible for the sleeves of Happy Mondays and James, amongst others). The show was a complete success, with an attendance of over 1600 attending. Neil then brought the exhibition to London from 20 November to 2 December. The exhibition consisted of twenty-three representations of comedians, which were originally painted in acrylics, blown-up, colour photo-copied and overlaid to produce the final image. The background music for the show was written by Bernard Sumner. Special T-shirts were on sale, and for the promotion Neil exclusively modelled an Arthur Askey creation.

Rounding off the year, PMI (Picture Music International) released *HIGHLIGHTS: Pet Shop Boys on Tour*, on 3 December, a selection of tracks filmed at Wembley Arena during the Boys' 1989 tour. The tracks included 'The Sound of the Atom Splitting', 'It's a Sin', 'Shopping', 'Love Comes Quickly', 'Domino Dancing', 'Rent', 'King's Cross' and 'It's Alright'.

Neil's hint to *New Musical Express* in September that in 1991 the Pet Shop Boys were going to tour Canada, USA, Australia, Japan and Britain – and take their shows a bit further – was confirmed by the record company when it stated that Neil and Chris would be undertaking their first-ever world tour, having finalized five UK dates for June 1991. The performances were to be directed by David Alden and designed by David Fielding, both of whom had worked extensively with the English National Opera. The record company said the Boys were planning an 'uncompromising event with few concessions to the presentation normally associated with a rock show'.

'We want to do it all completely differently. We want to take the concerts as far away from a rock gig as possible. Pop concerts can have a very dull image,' Neil told the *Star's* Linda Duff. 'I can guarantee it'll be totally new.'

The cycle was complete.

Epilogue

It has been a campaign to end all campaigns, regimented by precision timing, selective audiences, superlative packaging, not only of the Pet Shop Boys' product but themselves. Yet break down the wall of indifference, let the self-control slip, and we are given a glimpse of two entertaining figures, not cardboard cut-outs. Tennant, the comic, his sidekick Lowe with the wit to woo when he opens his mouth. The sincerity, so often hidden, is there, if people look for it.

Dance music, strongly influenced in its embryonic stage by Bobby Orlando, has been the stepping stone to the monumental success of Neil Tennant and Chris Lowe. Interpolations of hip-hop and Latin mix have helped fuel the tragi-discoesque feel, culminating at the disco door. The style has been one long contradiction, with uncompromising, semi-depressing lyrics augmented by hi-NRG synthesizer backdrops. It has also worked superbly well. It was always meant to be perfectly straightforward, but it was never looked on in that way. The irony, the cynicism, so often linked with the Boys, has often been lost on them, although they have made it all look so easy that the cynicism has crept in. There they are, humourless poseurs of the first degree, cultivating the mystique by their very aloofness, compounding the myth by manipulative discourse, with one finger held up to the rest of the world.

The Pet Shop Boys' whole career has been lived like a magician's act. You never quite know what surprise they are going to pull out of the hat next. From those early days on

'Top of the Pops', when their non-act won widespread approval from the audience, the Boys have managed to spring a refreshing lease of life into the pop market. And no matter how often they may say they have been misrepresented in the media, hardly anyone has a bad word to say against them. This, despite Barbara Windsor's 'darlings' never letting on whether it has all been genuine. Is there, in fact, irony lingering behind the melancholic music? It is mildly frustrating, but not enough to turn the listener off, or for the listener to turn the Boys off. That is their unique hold.

'When we started making records we didn't want to be like other pop groups. We always tried to have an image that was un-popstarish and quite stern. We also presented ourselves in a detached way so that we are not quite real in what we do,' says Tennant.

'We didn't want to be smiling, good-time party people, because we weren't interested in that kind of thing. We always want to do things totally differently.'

And so they did.

'We have this word we use,' says Neil. 'Tragic. When we say something is tragic, we mean corny and dreadful, like a lot of rock groups. We were always concerned that we wouldn't be tragic. The music business is so formalized now – they want all the groups to be the same, but we try not to be like everyone else.'

You have to admire their tenacity, their self-control. Yet catch him off-camera, and Chris will crack. He does smile – in private. But he doesn't like smiling if it's not natural and, to Chris, posing for a photograph is false. He did smile once on 'Top of the Pops'. 'But a real professional can be all nice on stage, and the minute you're off, can be horrible. That's what you call a pro. A lot of the things we do don't make you want to smile,' he believes.

Neil admits they are stroppy sometimes, but they don't throw that many tantrums. Sometimes to get what you want you have to, he says, but the Pet Shop Boys are perfectionists. 'We like it to be right, whether it's the sleeve design, the photographs or the music itself, and it's maddening and frustrating if it isn't.'

As an example, on one 'Top of the Pops' appearance, the audience was clapping so loudly that Neil could not hear the song and almost walked off in disgust. Says Chris, 'You get some pop stars who just love to be on stage in front of an audience. I've never got much of a buzz off that. The first time we had to perform we just stood there and did the song, and that's how we've always done it. I can't think of anything else we could do, really. Maybe I could dance, but I'd feel like an idiot.'

Tennant, loaded down with the persona of world-weariness, tugging along Lowe in his wake, worked on their image, and the public took the bait. They grabbed it with both hands as the music justified the means. Some people, believes Neil, like their lives to be a soap opera. 'But if you're seriously committed to your work and have integrity in what you do, you don't really want that sort of thing. A group like Bros, who are so recognizable, are followed everywhere, but the pressure of fame isn't enormous on us,' he says.

'I think you have to be incredibly attractive for that to happen. I don't know that people have a sexual interest in us. Our pictures might be on a lot of people's walls, but they don't like us because they think we're good looking. We don't really know who our fans are. We seem to have a wide age range and we get a lot of boys writing in. But they like us because of the music. They know there's more of a purpose than being a pin-up. And our songs aren't just banal pop songs.'

'We do have suspicions about touring. Both of us feel that lots of concerts we see are boring,' admits Neil. 'When I was at *Smash Hits*, if any rock journalist was put on the rack and you turned it a few ratchets he'd admit that nearly every show he'd seen was boring. It's great when they come on and for the first few minutes you think, Oh wow, this is fab. And then a couple of minutes later you're bored to tears, the sound's awful and all the journalists are in the bar gossiping, which is far more fun.

'Besides, groups do change on the road and the demands of a big, live audience can change and vulgarize your music. Eurythmics would probably disagree with me but I personally think their music has changed for the worse. They started off as a pervy synth duo and I really liked their records. She [Annie Lennox] was a good singer and they did their own videos, which they seem to have stopped now. But something seems to happen when you hit big in America. People feel they can't get away with being a pervy synth duo and they've got to have a proper rock drummer and backing singers, and suddenly they've got a different sounding set of songs. And so the next album reflects that change.

'It's a great cliché of rock journalism when an artist tells you, "Our new album represents what the band sounds like live nowadays, which is a lot harder and tougher"; i.e., they've become a rock 'n' roll cliché – ironically of course – and I think this is where people lose the thread of the plot.'

The Pet Shop Boys never set out to be cult figures, but that is how they have ended up, particularly on the dance floor. And, contrary to popular myth in some quarters, the success has not been solely charted by Tennant. He says the group's attitude has been set much more by Lowe, who has a completely different way of looking at things. As different as chalk and cheese. Lowe, ever ready to put his foot down and say no when the necessity arose. Not as a child might throw a tantrum in the supermarket, but as an accomplished musician with intelligent ideas, away from the rock 'n' roll syndrome: a refreshing outsider's view. Never mind if this annoyed Tennant; he would always listen.

They have steered their own course, away from the rock circus which they say weakens everything, waters it down. *'You wanna be in my gang . . .'* sang Gary Glitter. 'No thank you' say the Boys, in particular Chris. That is why they have never appeared on a compilation album. That is why they refused to become involved in the Steven Spielberg movie.

'I hate pop gangs!' says Chris. 'When we went to see Madonna, I loathed being surrounded by all those pop people in the special enclosure; I'd far rather have been out front with everybody else. It's really embarrassing – you've got this strange relationship with people you recognize, like Bob Geldof. You know them and they know you from the papers or the telly, but you don't really because you've never been introduced, and you don't know whether to nod or not. It makes me cringe. I hate the idea of us being part of the whole pop thing, even though we are.'

'We don't really say horrible things about other people any more,' Chris continues. 'It's best to say them privately, as there's nothing worse than saying something awful about a group and then bumping into them.'

'The Human League taught us something very interesting and that was to avoid meeting other pop stars because it's easier to continue hating their records. Suppose you really, really hated Genesis records. You just happen to meet Phil Collins and he's about the nicest person you could ever hope to meet,' says Chris. 'We don't take drugs, there are no groupies and we're not back-slapping with Spandau Ballet, Simply Red, Duran Duran and whoever else might be around.'

Like two carnivores, they have gnawed away at the pop industry, taking the richest pickings and leaving the rest for other chart-busters to squabble over. It's almost as if it's been one, drawn-out yawn, though. It has also been a major selling point. They have cultivated this mystique by not becoming involved. 'Obviously we don't want to be over-exposed and it's a way of avoiding that,' says Neil. 'You know what Boy George said about Prince; "It's good he doesn't do interviews because when you meet him you realize he's a boring, normal person. He's a muso who can dance." We didn't necessarily set out to gain mystique, but what we definitely set out not to do from the beginning was to present ourselves as a jolly pop group on the back page of *Jackie*.

'Being in a pop group isn't about being presented as two real people. It's about the Pet Shop Boys, and you know what you want to look like so it's important to keep up with vetting all the photos. Not necessarily because you want to look cosmetically beautiful, but because you don't want some half-witted shot of you grinning like a pop group. That's what it's all about. Yes, of course, we have a strong idea of what image we want presented to the public.

'People get watered down in this business, but when we do something we know exactly what we want, otherwise we wouldn't do it. Like the covers of our records: someone told our designer they were amazed how we got away with the cover of *Please*, because it was so uncompromising – a tiny little photo on a huge white sleeve. But EMI trust our instincts.'

Says Neil, 'You've got to pay attention to everything because if you don't think of something, nobody else will necessarily think of it for you. So even when we're away we're checking to see that the fly posters have been put up and that the record artwork is OK, because the visual thing is such an important part of us.'

The Pet Shop Boys never had a long-term aim, purely short-term goals. They claimed the points without paying the penalty or sacrificing their individuality. As Tennant says, in pop music you can pretend to be something and if you do it well, you will be successful at what you're pretending to be. 'George Michael decides he wants to make it in America as a mature solo artist, so he very sensibly sits down and says, right, I'm going to make a record with a guitar in it, because everyone says you've got to play the guitar and have a drummer to make it big in America. And he does it. And he wears a leather jacket as well, and in the video he plays a guitar and the record goes to Number One in America. And *Rolling Stone* magazine has a cover feature which says what a marvellous, mature performer he is nowadays. It's astonishing really.

'And U2 do videos rather mysteriously in black and white and they all look very serious so you assume the song has got some content. But you'd never get U2 singing a song called "Let's Make Lots of Money". That would express some kind of irony or feeling about the music industry,' says Tennant.

Madonna, he feels, is a real disco artist, her songs relaying totally simple things, like "Holiday" and "Celebrate". They are mostly straightforward love songs, but it's the feeling they give off. Is he saying, then, that the Pet Shop Boys are not real disco artists? If he is, he is right. Tennant and Lowe come in at a completely different angle. It's the music that has the impetus to project them on to the floor, not the lyrics. They are anything but simplistic. Like it or not, Tennant is somewhat of a political animal. 'Shopping' is a prime example. Says Tennant: 'That's about selling off nationalized industries. They had that grisly "Tell Sid" campaign. When we were doing the demos for the album, everywhere you went there was this fucking "Tell Sid". Not only do they sell off nationalized industries, but they have to patronize the entire country while they do it. God, that "Tell Sid" thing. We used to be apoplectic with rage. I was thrilled when it all collapsed. Absolutely thrilled to pieces.'

'We don't present ourselves as a political group. In many ways there's nothing more embarrassing than pop stars talking about politics. No matter how deeply rooted one's political feelings are, and a lot of people in pop groups are socialists, probably wet liberal socialists – you, me and Simon Le Bon all want to keep the NHS going – we're all basically saying the same thing, and after a bit it sounds banal. People don't realize they're just saying what everybody is thinking anyway and they're talking down to people as well. So in the past we've tended to avoid those sorts of issues and people tend not to ask us about them anyway because that's not what the Pet Shop Boys are about.'

At the other end of the spectrum, 'Always on my Mind' is a particularly moving song, and one which Tennant enjoys singing. 'I know some people think it's about a jerk. I thought it was someone making excuses. It's someone who assumed – actually it's quite an English idea – that they didn't have to express their love because they assumed that the other person assumed that they were both in love. And then he realizes that he or she or whatever didn't assume that, and he's surprised. So that's what I thought about when I sang it.

"Heart", too, is just completely straightforward. I mean, it could be a Madonna song.'

In a cynical sense, it has been easy to read the lyrics behind the lyrics. To expose something that is not there, but that you would like to be. 'Rent', for example, was naturally presumed to be about rent boys, and behind the mirth sneaks in a touch of cynicism from Tennant, who actually admits, 'I suppose in some of our songs we're a little cynical. I mean, we deliberately take ideas like "Rent" – and you think, God, that's controversial because everyone will think it's about rent boys – but it won't be about rent boys. I suppose that's where the cynicism comes in. But then actually writing the song, it changes.

'In "Rent", I always imagine that I am singing the woman's part. It's set in New York, and it's about a kept woman, kept by someone very powerful – a senator or someone like that. The affair has been going on for twenty years and she's suddenly thinking, what's she got out of it? Did she make the wrong decision from the start when she fell for this guy? She could have had a job or a family, but instead she has this apartment and a guy comes around twice a week. But then she thinks, well, it could have been worse. We do love each other. We do have a relationship. It has lasted. I love you and, you know, you pay the rent. It's the compromise of life. That's something. I suppose, that comes out when I write lyrics.'

In fact, Tennant sees marriage as a compromise, not that he has ever been faced with that situation. For many, it pays off in the end. Even that, though, he sees as a form of cynicism – the very idea of making do with something, rather than trying to achieve the absolute ideal. The cynicism arises because it assumes that one knows things are not perfect in the first place. Sincerity has its niche in the order of the Pet Shop Boys' tree of life. The album *Please* is a good example. The songs are placed in order, beginning with two people running away; the excitement is engendered. They make it to the big city ('West End Girls') and onward to the night-club scene ('Tonight is Forever').

The Pet Shop Boys play across the musical spectrum, and have attracted a wide audience because of it. The teenies digest the music, and the adults chew over the words. 'Why Don't We Live Together', from the *Please* album, is for the maturer generation: the 'thirtysomethings' who see the drawing of realization and sense behind the way their parents have lived their lives.

Says Tennant: 'They lived a smaller life and it wasn't glamorous and it wasn't in a huge city, but they're still together. They still, apparently, are happy. And you think, my God, I may never end up that happy. Or that there are worse things.'

Tennant, five years Lowe's senior, grew up in the Newcastle suburbs under an umbrella of boredom and implicit violence. His adolescence was wrapped around the skinhead era. Fortunately, he was never at the receiving end of their boots, although he knew people subjected to such thuggery. And it stayed with him. Thus we have 'Suburbia' and 'Violence' on the first album. This socio-consciousness is prevalent through most of their work, and personified in the film *It Couldn't Happen Here*. Sadly, the film turned out to be such a nonsense that any serious intentions were lost as the viewer lost interest. As a vehicle for their videos, it worked well, but one would have preferred less of the spoof, which acted more as a detraction than as a vehicle for understanding.

I warmed to Chris Lowe in the film. It was as if he was merely along for the ride, although he never looked like an out-and-out apology. He was probably inwardly smiling to himself. No one can blame him for that. And luckily enough the film, despite its poor reviews, did not damage their reputations. It certainly did nothing to enhance them, either. If it had been brought out at the same time as the Beatles and the Monkeys were into making movies, more would have been read into it, but for all Jack Bond's intents, it fell on stoney ground. But the Pets survived. When the film made it into the video shops, you had to put your advance order in to hire it out. Chris Lowe would have liked that. This most private of people once said, 'Even if we wanted to, we'd never be big stars. We have no star quality. We're the kind of people nobody remembers. At school, not a single teacher managed to remember my name.' Having said that, he was not looking for the sympathy vote. He has always preferred it that way.

According to Lowe, the Pet Shop Boys became popular through their honesty. 'We are who we are, and we don't try to be anything else, which is rare these days. So we get lots of fan letters, all of which Neil corrects and returns to sender. Having worked as assistant editor [*Smash Hits*], he can't stand spelling mistakes.'

Melancholic and aloof on stage, relaxed and witty off it, the Pet Shop Boys are a dichotomy. Tennant, coming across as the thinking man's pop star; Lowe playing the role of the *dauphin*. Popsters with a degree in absenteeism – but only when it suits them. Their mock inventiveness has seen them flourish where others would have quickly foundered. They have dodged the pop clichés, yet adorned themselves with exhilarating crescendos of electronically generated sound – breaking through the barrier with complex, robotic-sounding production studio technology and masterful trickery. And they capitalized on it at the right time. The studio sound was studio bound, and there was nobody to challenge the supremacy of their art. They set a precedent, and that is why they are where they are today. And deservedly so. Pop House, acid House, with its synco-pated, techno, pre-sequenced rhythms, is now all to the fore. The studio children, the 4-track, bedsit solo artists are suddenly all coming out to play. Backed by a myriad of computers. To see some acts on 'Top of the Pops' is an embarrassment. It's high treason to the Musicians' Union, whose motto is 'Keep Music Live'. After each elongated sequence of notes, another pre-programmed key will be touched, and off they go again. This digital diligence is an easy option and does nothing for the audience whatsoever. All the artist can do is smile embarrassedly, apologetically at the camera. The spontaneity of the music is lost forever. The public is at the mercy of the mainframe. Load in the wrong disc, and the performer has had it.

The Pet Shop Boys knew the pitfalls of appearing live, that is why they remained behind closed doors for so long. They knew they had to do more on stage than simply be there. Exposed to the harsh reality of live work they knew would reveal their limitations. And they weren't afraid to admit it. They wanted more than stagecraft. They needed witchcraft to make it work to their advantage. It did. To many people they were brilliant, as the imagery enhanced their music. They endeavoured to bring their music to life through that imagery. They also tried to maintain their sincerity. It was not a happy mix. Because the Pet Shop Boys throughout their brief career had always tried to under-sell themselves. Suddenly they were in the shop window, for all to view. The over-sell and the over-kill. It was full marks to them for trying – and bringing it off – something they will likely do again. But it doesn't matter. It's their music that has always been most important, not personal appearances. 'Playing live isn't a natural thing for us to do,' says Neil. 'Chris and I came together as song-writers and then we made records – it's not like we're a band who got spotted by talent scouts.'

No one knows the Pet Shop Boys better than themselves. Neil Tennant, journalist turned pop star, would have hated to interview them. 'We don't do many photo sessions and we refuse to fall in with all the ideas magazines suggest for features. I would have found us difficult and big-headed,' he notes.

For someone who looks upon success as a rather crass concept, Tennant would never take the latter for granted. 'I suppose we're really rather passive; we accept it, we think, Oh, great. I'm not putting it down – I think it's fantastic and I sort of think we deserve it, but I also have the feeling that you appreciate it more afterwards.'

Masquerading behind their masks of moodiness, the Pet Shop Boys are in reality two very private, hard-working, amiable perfectionists. The world can huff, and it can puff, and it can blow away to its heart's content about their music, their sexuality, their personas, but, frankly, my dears, they couldn't give a damn.

'Will we become divorced from reality the more successful we become?' Neil queried in 1987. 'Firstly, most of that is a myth. Secondly, you actually have to desire it. You've got to work incredibly hard to set yourself completely apart from the rest of the world. People say to me, "Oh, you're the geezer from the Pet Shop Boys, aren't you?" Sometimes I deny it, but whenever I admit it, inevitably they go, "No you're not." You can't win.'

Yet, the Pet Shop Boys have won. They established the ground rules, played the game, scaled the ladder until they were eye-level with success. And they achieved it without compromise. Without giving anything away. Faceless people in the pop machinery regurgitating the same arguments in order to retain their privacy and, thus, their individuality.

One cannot help but admire them for that. We almost saw the light when their names were proposed as personalities to switch on the illuminations in Chris's home town of Blackpool. Consternation and bewilderment swept through the chamber as several councillors queried, 'Who?'

Nice one, Boys.

Notes and Sources

In the course of my research for this biography, many potential subjects who I approached were either reluctant to open up in the first instance, or refused point blank to go on record about the Pet Shop Boys, their personal lives or their music. In rare instances, interviewees have insisted on complete anonymity, and I have respected the wishes of the individuals concerned.

On various occasions during the writing of the book, I made earnest approaches to interview Neil Tennant and Chris Lowe, through the press office of Parlophone Records, Massive Management, and through Jill Wall, who now runs the duo's management office. On each occasion I was denied access to them, on the grounds that they had no desire to be involved with the biography.

The comments, therefore, of Chris Lowe and Neil Tennant have been culled from interviews the duo have given to various publications since their successful rise in the music world, and I am indebted to those publications which kindly granted me permission to reproduce the material here.

For the sake of clarity, in the following section I have duplicated source material whenever I felt it necessary to do so. Publication dates have also been included. Other quotes from the duo and various other personalities have been taken from press release material. Whenever practical, sources have been mentioned in the body of the text.

The following notes are chronologically listed, chapter by chapter, to act as a guide to the identity of the sources used by me. All quotes, from whatever source, have been reproduced in good faith. All quotes unlisted were given to me in personal interviews.

Prologue

Lowe was happy to admit . . . to get on with: Roald Rynning for *Biz*, 19 July 1987.
Obviously people are going . . .': Neil Tennant in an interview with Roald Rynning for *Biz*, 19 July 1987.

Chapter One

'We sent Susan to piano . . .': Bill Tennant to the *Sunday Sun*, Newcastle, 26 January 1986.
'My major clothes time . . .': Neil Tennant to Mark Booker, writing for *Number One*, 5 July 1989.
'I couldn't afford . . .': Neil Tennant to Mark Booker.
'I had short hair . . .': Neil Tennant in conversation with Mark Booker.
'The first interview I did . . .': Neil Tennant in an interview with Paul Mathur for *Melody Maker*, 27 February 1986
'When I used to proof . . .': Neil Tennant to *Biz*, 19 July 1987.

Chapter Two

'All I remember are topless . . .': Chris Lowe in conversation with Roald Rynning for *Biz*, 19 July 1987.
'I always tried to wear . . .': Chris Lowe to Mark Booker for *Number One*, 5 July 1989.
'I had only one dream . . .': Chris Lowe to *Biz*, 19 July 1987.
'Our musical tastes . . .': Chris Lowe to the *Sun*, 17 January 1986.

'It started as a hobby really . . .': Chris Lowe to the *Evening Gazette*, Blackpool, 13 December 1985.

'Every time we went in . . .': Neil Tennant in conversation with David Wigg for *DX* magazine, September 1988.

'We were convinced . . .': Chris Lowe to Paul Mathur, *Melody Maker*, 22 February 1986.

Chapter Three

'He's three years older than me . . .': Neil Tennant to the *Evening Chronicle*, Newcastle, 2 May 1984.

Chapter Four

'Meeting Bobby O . . .': Neil Tennant to the *Evening Chronicle*, Newcastle, 2 May 1984.

'We learned a lot . . .': Neil Tennant to the *Evening Chronicle*.

'It was a risk leaving . . .': Neil Tennant to the *Daily Express*, 17 January 1986.

'I must be mad . . .': Neil Tennant to *Biz*, 19 July 1987.

'I don't miss it . . .': Neil Tennant to *Biz*.

'My mum always told me . . .': Chris Lowe to the *Evening Standard*, 10 April 1984.

'A new duo, who go under . . .': *Evening Standard* report, 10 April 1984.

Chapter Eight

'I'm on the first rung . . .': Belouis Some to the *Daily Express*, 31 January 1986.

'The song was released...': Neil Tennant to the *Daily Express*, 17 January 1986.

'They were thrilled and amazed...': Parlophone spokesman as reported in the *Evening Chronicle*, Newcastle, 11 January 1986.

'It's a brilliant song...': Neil Tennant to the *Daily Mirror*, 15 January 1986.

Chapter Nine

'We were appearing at...': Neil Tennant to the *Daily Mirror*, 8 January 1986.

'Meeting him three years later...': Neil Tennant to the *Daily Mirror*.

'I thought at least they would...': Chris Lowe in conversation with the *Sun*'s 'Bizarre' columnist, 14 January 1986.

'It's strange because I think...': Chris Lowe in the *Evening Gazette*, Blackpool, 18 January 1986.

'Both of us liked it...': Chris Lowe to the *Evening Gazette*.

'They really offered a fortune...': Neil Tennant to the *Daily Mirror*'s Linda Duff, 15 June 1987.

'I like to be anonymous...': Chris Lowe to the *Evening Gazette*, 18 January 1986.

'You do so much of it...': Chris Lowe in the *Evening Gazette*.

'Pop music has never been about...': Neil Tennant to David Hancock of the *Sun*'s 'Bizarre' column, 17 January 1986.

'The trouble is there is not enough...': Chris Lowe to David Hancock.

'Sometimes I think maybe we...': Neil Tennant in conversation with the *Sun*'s David Hancock.

'I heard that because we...': Neil Tennant told Paul Mathur of *Melody Maker*, 22 February 1986.

'They are both very . . .': Neil Tennant in the *Sun*, 17 January 1986.

'At St Cuthbert's School, where the music . . .': Bill Tennant to the *Sunday Sun*, Newcastle, 26 January 1986.

'Since his record got in the charts . . .': Neil's father Bill to the *Sunday Sun*.

'And anyone familiar . . .' a report in the *Evening Standard*, 3 February 1986.

'Oh God, you're not going to . . .': A Parlophone Records spokesman to the *Evening Standard*, 3 February 1986.

'One of the newspapers said . . .': Neil Tennant to Paul Mathur in *Melody Maker*, 22 February 1986.

'It's funny but we've got a knack . . .' (Lowe); 'This tour's just for promotional . . .' (Tennant); 'If we wanted to be big in Italy . . .' (Lowe) 'A lot of things happen in Italy . . .' (Lowe); 'When I started on *Smash Hits* . . .' (Tennant); 'It's not the slightest bit difficult . . .' (Tennant); '. . . the sort of attitude when . . .' (Tennant); 'All that "loved your new style" . . .' (Tennant); from an interview with Paul Mathur, *Melody Maker*, 22 February 1986.

Chapter Ten

'Tennant's voice is remarkably like . . .': *Evening Gazette*, 5 April 1986.

It contributed to the sexual ambiguity played on by the duo . . .: a report in *Record Collector*, Issue No. 89, January 1987.

'EMI's pet pop duo . . .': Jeremy Lewis in the *Sunday Express*, 6 April 1986.

It won't be the usual . . .': *Daily Mirror*, 5 May 1986.

'It's important to make records . . .': Neil Tennant to Paul Mathur, *Melody Maker*, 22 February 1986.

'It's like those stupid . . .': Neil Tennant to Paul Mathur.

'The Pet Shop Boys would love to be . . .': Paul Mathur.

'We played this TV show . . .': Neil Tennant in conversation with Paul Mathur.

'When we first came over to America . . .': Neil Tennant in an interview with Andrew Sullivan for *Sky* magazine, September 1988.

'I used to have jobs like . . .': Chris Lowe to Andrew Sullivan for *Sky*.

'We haven't performed much before . . .': Chris Lowe to the *Evening Gazette*, Blackpool, 16 January 1986.

Chapter Eleven

'We didn't want to do . . .'; 'We did something quite literal . . .'; 'I like the bit with Chris . . .'; 'I don't want us to make . . .'; 'It's the thing you see . . .'; 'I think the video as a whole . . .': Neil Tennant to Paul Mathur for *Melody Maker* on the video compilation, *Television*, 3 January 1987.

'. . . hated being judged . . .': Chris Lowe to Linda Duff, *Daily Mirror*, 15 June 1987.

'I find I can get carried away . . .': Neil Tennant to Linda Duff.

'You can't do this to him . . .': Siouxsie, of Siouxsie and the Banshees, as reported by Martin Townsend for *Today*, 11 February 1987.

'The security people . . .': record company spokesman to Martin Townsend.

'The record companies . . .': spokesman for Showsec Security to Martin Townsend.

Chapter Twelve

'It's the duo's most obvious . . .': *Evening Gazette*, Blackpool, 20 June 1987.

'Frankly, it's rather embarrassing . . .': Neil Tennant to Linda Duff, *Daily Mirror*, 16 June 1987.

'We have made a lot of money . . .'; 'People tend to think . . .': Neil Tennant to the *Daily Mirror*, 19 June 1987.

'It's fantastic, really great . . .': Neil Tennant to Tim Pedley, *Evening Chronicle*, Newcastle, 2 July 1987.

'Just because you're at Number One . . .': *Evening News*, 3 July 1987.

'Chris is a very moody person . . .': *Evening News*, 3 July 1987.

'It's an unusual subject . . .': Neil Tennant to Tim Pedley, *Evening Chronicle*, Newcastle, 2 July 1987.

'That doesn't mean . . .'; 'We went along there . . .'; 'A lot of people expect . . .'; 'What it is that . . .'; 'They're ones that I'm sure . . .'; 'It's funny, but you still . . .': Neil Tennant in an interview with Scott Lebris for *Sky* magazine, 18 June 1987.

'I was very impressed . . .': Neil Tennant to David Wigg for *DX* magazine, 17 September 1988.

'I thought I wanted to be . . .'; 'When I was growing up . . .': Neil Tennant to Linda Duff, *Daily Mirror*, 15 June 1987.

'It is very unfortunate that Neil . . .': Teacher from St Cuthbert's to the *Evening Chronicle*, Newcastle, 27 July 1987.

'There was a lot of . . .': Chris Baines to Simon Malia for *Mercury East Midlands*, Nottingham, 26 July 1987, and as reported in the *Evening Chronicle*, Newcastle, 27 July 1987.

'I think the school . . .': Neil's mum Sheila to the *Sunday Sun*, Newcastle, 27 December 1987.

Neil revealed at this time . . .: Neil Tennant in conversation with Tim Pedley for the *Evening Chronicle*, Newcastle, 2 July 1987.

'Producers can make you . . .': Chris Lowe to the *Daily Mirror*, 7 July 1987.

'We've never been about sleaze . . .': Chris Lowe in conversation with Daniela Soave for *Sky* magazine, 24 September 1987.

'We have the same attitude . . .': Neil Tennant to Daniela Soave for *Sky*.

'When it comes to rock music . . .'; 'We basically reject the pomp . . .'; 'Too many pop bands . . .': David Ball of Soft Cell, interviewed by *US* magazine, 25 April 1983.

'At a time when it is said . . .'; 'It will be interesting . . .': a report in *Record Collector*, Issue No. 89, January 1987.

Chapter Thirteen

'We wanted a woman . . .'; 'Her breathy, glamourous voice . . .': Neil Tennant to the *Sunday Times*, 9 August 1987.

'We weren't sure . . .': Neil Tennant to the *Sunday Times*, 9 August 1987.

'Chris, Stephen and I . . .'; 'No one's interested . . .': Neil Tennant in the *Sunday Times*, 9 August 1987 (copyright © Times Newspapers Ltd, 1987).

'The producer didn't understand . . .': Neil Tennant in conversation with Roald Rynning for *Biz*, 19 July 1987.

'We think the single . . .': Neil Tennant to the *Star*, 7 August 1987.

'They (Neil and Chris) also believe . . .': the *Sun*, 22 July 1987.

Chapter Fourteen

'Everything Madonna does . . .': Neil Tennant to Daniela Soave for *Sky* magazine, 24 September 1987.

'We didn't want to be . . .': Neil and Chris in conversation with Sheryl Garratt for *News on Sunday*, 1 November 1987.

'Awkward, miserable bastards . . .': as admitted to Sheryl Garratt in *News on Sunday*, 1 November 1987.

'If it has our name on it . . .' (Chris Lowe); 'I thought the cover . . .' (Neil Tennant) to Sheryl Garratt.

'It is tremendously exciting . . .': Sheila Tennant to Neil McKay, *Sunday Sun*, Newcastle, 27 December 1987.

'They have proved all it takes . . .': the *Sun*, 29 December 1987.

Chapter Fifteen

'We met Jack for dinner . . .' (Chris Lowe); 'The first thing . . .' (Neil Tennant); 'It's very English . . .' (Neil Tennant); 'The film is very British . . .' (Chris Lowe); 'It's an episodic film . . .' (film director, Jack Bond); 'They're so unstarry . . .' (Jack Bond); 'I'm a nervous wreck . . .' (Neil Tennant); as reported to David Toop for a feature on the Pet Shop Boys' film, *It Couldn't Happen Here*, in the *Sunday Times*, 3 July 1988 (copyright © Times Newspapers Ltd, 1988).

'I only agreed . . .': actor Joss Ackland to the *Sun*.

'Eventually, we had to . . .': Neil Tennant to Sheryl Garratt, *News on Sunday*, 1 November 1987.

Chapter Sixteen

'Chris Lowe was not dressed . . .': Glynn Watson; 'The dress rules . . .' (Ken Buckley); According to Chris's mother Vivien: a report in the *Evening Gazette*, Blackpool, 29 December 1987.

'It's kind of macho nowadays . . .': Neil Tennant to Jon Wall for *Time Out*, 12 to 19 July 1989.

'To an extent the award . . .': the *Star*, 13 July 1988.

'Neil wasn't happy . . .': Patsy Kensit to Annette Witheridge for the *Star*, 18 March 1988.

'I think she's got quite . . .': Neil Tennant to Daniela Soave for *Sky*, 24 September 1987.

'We're taking this stand . . .': Woolworth spokesman, the *Sun*, 22 April 1988.

'It's come as a complete surprise . . .'; 'It's brilliant to . . .': Neil Tennant to Deirdre Fernard for the *Sunday Times* magazine, 10 July 1988 (copyright © Times Newspapers Ltd, 1988).

'They call themselves . . .': Neil Tennant, the *Star*, 20 September 1988.

'This may sound like a minor point . . .'; 'A very famous . . .': Chris Lowe in the *Evening Gazette*, Blackpool, 17 September 1988.

'Let's face it, we're not a band . . .': Neil Tennant to *News on Sunday*, 25 April 1988.

'Pop music has never been . . .': Neil Tennant to Annette Witheridge for the *Star*, 29 November 1988.

Chapter Seventeen

'It's because you wail . . .': Neil Tennant about Liza Minnelli to David Quantick for *New Musical Express*, 19 August 1989.

'The only thing I was looking for . . .'; 'Chemical dependency is a . . .'; 'But those feelings have to be accepted . . .': Liza Minnelli in conversation with Andrew Billen for the *Observer* magazine, 13 August 1989.

'They almost had these Gregorian . . .'; 'They've always just treated me . . .': Liza Minnelli to David Quantick in *New Musical Express*.

'Liza is fabulous . . .': Neil Tennant in the *Observer* magazine.

'I went to a lot of friends . . .': Liza Minnelli in *Smash Hits*, 23 August to 5 September 1989.

'When I first came to London . . .'; 'This was just before . . .' (Neil Tennant); 'What I always look for . . .'; 'They really pushed me . . .' (Liza Minnelli); 'A lot of it is quite sexy . . .'; 'I always maintain . . .' (Neil Tennant); 'That first time I met . . .' (Liza Minnelli) to David Quantick.

'I'd wanted to make a rock record . . .': Liza Minnelli to Andrew Billen.

'The thrilling thing is . . .'; 'Chris's attitude is so great . . .': Liza Minnelli to David Quantick.

Chapter Eighteen

'I'm not getting involved . . .' (Jimmy Tarbuck); 'It was over a silly thing . . .' (Neil Tennant): the *Star*, 7 March 1989.

'He said we were . . .': Neil Tennant to the *Independent*, 25 February 1988.

'We want it to be spectacular . . .': Chris Lowe, *Daily Mirror*, 27 October 1989.

'It's taken a lot of heart-searching . . .': Neil Tennant, the *Sun*, 4 December 1989.

'I have done everything else . . .': Derek Jarman, *Daily Mirror*, 31 May 1989.

'Neil says he's sometimes . . .': Derek Jarman on Neil Tennant in an interview with *City Limits*, 1989.

'This is the tour . . .': Neil Tennant and Chris Lowe, *Evening Gazette*, Blackpool, 10 June 1989.

'It's almost like being . . .'; 'We wanted an empty . . .' (Chris Lowe); 'Our claim to fame . . .'; 'I've always wanted . . .' (Neil Tennant): in conversation with Mark Cooper, the *Guardian*, 7 July 1989.

'Even at that time . . .'; 'Previously our management . . .'; 'We felt a bit sneaky . . .'; 'He was on the phone to us . . .'; 'From the outset . . .' (Neil Tennant); 'The reasons why we didn't play live . . .' (Chris Lowe): in an interview with Jon Wall, *Time Out*, 12 to 19 July 1989.

'It was exciting . . .': Neil Tennant, *Smash Hits*, 12 to 25 July 1989.

'Yes, I think we were both . . .': Neil Tennant to Jon Wall.

'I'd prefer it to be a one-off . . .': Chris Lowe to *Smash Hits*, 12 to 25 July 1989.

'Neil was on a high' : as reported by Chris Heath in his book, *Pet Shop Boys, Actually* (Viking, 1990).

'The whole show . . .' (Neil Tennant); '. . . not only have we done . . .' (Neil Tennant and Chris Lowe); 'I had to keep thinking . . .' (Neil Tennant): *Smash Hits*, 12 to 25 July 1989.

'He was speechless at first . . .' (Insider); 'I certainly got the baby bug . . .' (Neil Tennant): report on a video shoot, the *Star*, 19 June 1989.

'The problem was that we didn't . . .'; 'It'll be totally different . . .'; 'We always knew that . . .'; 'I don't mind having . . .': Neil Tennant to Mark Booker, *Number One*, 5 July 1989.

'Sometimes, we've been puzzled . . .': Neil Tennant to Jon Wall, *Time Out*, July 1989.

Chris Lowe suddenly made his excuses . . .: as reported in the *Daily Mirror*, September 1989.

Chapter Twenty-one

'We wanted to get away a bit . . .': Chris Lowe to Stuart Maconie in *New Musical Express*, 22 September 1990.

'. . . appear to have been at the pruning sheers . . .': Roger Morton, *New Musical Express*, 22 September 1990.

'We are quite pessimistic people . . .': Neil Tennant, *Smash Hits*, 19 September to 2 October 1990.

'We want to do it all . . .': Neil Tennant to Linda Duff, the *Star*, 23 August 1990.

Epilogue

'When we started . . .': Neil Tennant to David Wigg, *DX*, 17 September 1988.

'We have this word we use . . .' (Neil Tennant); 'But a real professional . . .' (Chris Lowe); 'We like it to be right . . .' (Neil Tennant); 'You get some pop stars . . .' (Chris Lowe); 'But if you're seriously committed . . .'; 'I think you have to be . . .'

(Neil Tennant): as reported to Victoria Freedman, *Woman*, 9 July 1988.

'We do have suspicions . . .' (Neil Tennant); 'I hate pop gangs . . .' (Chris Lowe): to Kris Kirk, *Melody Maker*, 3 October 1987.

'We don't really say horrible . . .': Chris Lowe to Victoria Freedman, *Woman*, 3 October 1987.

'The Human League taught us . . .': Chris Lowe to Linda Duff, *Daily Mirror*, 15 June 1987.

'Obviously we don't want to be . . .'; 'You've got to pay attention . . .': Neil Tennant to Kris Kirk, *Melody Maker*, 3 October 1987.

'George Michael decides . . .'; 'That's about selling off . . .': Neil Tennant to Andrew Sullivan, *Sky*, September 1988.

'We don't present ourselves . . .': Neil Tennant, *Melody Maker*, 3 October 1987.

'I know some people think . . .'; 'I suppose in some of our songs . . .'; 'They lived a smaller life . . .': Neil Tennant to Andrew Sullivan, *Sky*, September 1988.

'Even if we wanted to . . .' (Chris Lowe); 'We are who we are . . .' (Neil Tennant): to Roald Rynning, *Biz*, 17 July 1987.

'Playing live isn't a natural thing . . .': Neil Tennant to Victoria Freedman, *Woman*, 9 July 1987.

'We don't do many photo sessions ..': Neil Tennant to Roald Rynning, *Biz*, 19 July 1987.

'I suppose we're really rather . . .'; 'Will we become divorced . . .': Neil Tennant to Daniela Soave, *Sky*, 24 September 1987.

Discography

UK 7-inch Singles

'WEST END GIRLS'/'PET SHOP BOYS' (Epic Records Cat: A 4292). Released: April 1984
'OPPORTUNITIES (LET'S MAKE LOTS OF MONEY)'/'IN THE NIGHT' (Parlophone Records Cat: R 6097). Released: 1 July 1985
'WEST END GIRLS'/'A MAN COULD GET ARRESTED' (Parlophone Cat: R 6115). Released: 28 October 1985. Picture disc released December 1985 Cat: RP 6115
'LOVE COMES QUICKLY'/'THAT'S MY IMPRESSION' (Parlophone Cat: R 6116). Released: 24 February 1986
'OPPORTUNITIES'/'WAS THAT WHAT IT WAS?' (Parlophone Cat: R 6129). Released: 19 May 1986
'SUBURBIA'/'PANINARO' (Parlophone Cat: R 6140). Released: 22 September 1986
'IT'S A SIN'/'YOU KNOW WHERE YOU WENT WRONG' (Parlophone Cat: R 6158). Released: 15 June 1987
'WHAT HAVE I DONE TO DESERVE THIS?'/'A NEW LIFE' (Parlophone Cat: R 6163). Released: 10 August 1987
'RENT'/'I WANT A DOG' (Parlophone Cat: R 6168). Released: 12 October 1987
'ALWAYS ON MY MIND'/'DO I HAVE TO?' (Parlophone Cat: R 6171). Released: 30 November 1987
'HEART'/'I GET EXCITED (YOU GET EXCITED TOO)' (Parlophone Cat: R 6177). Released: 21 March 1988